主 编 奚挺 吴晟

DETAILED IELTS

"低碳 雅思" 系列

口语 冲刺 Speaking

U0127736

浙江教育出版社

前　言

　　当读者们拿起这本书的时候,"低碳雅思"的名字或许会让人产生些许疑惑。其实这个名字既在意料之外,也在情理之中。当初在给这批系列书籍确定名称的时候,是费了很大的脑筋的。因为关于雅思考试的参考书籍,市面上并不缺乏,也各有风格,然而在编撰书稿的时候,我们首先想到的并不是要让这批书体现出怎样的风格,而是要让它从根本上契合雅思考试的出发点、细节:雅思考试主办方最为重视的,就是考生对细节信息的理解和表达能力。所以我们首先想到的,是一个朴实无华的英文名字,"Detailed IELTS",它实在是对这批书籍再实在不过的解读。而巧合的是,这个英文名的谐音恰恰就成了"低碳雅思"。"低碳"是一个全新的生活理念,它清新、干净,还与时俱进,于是我们就采用了这个名称,也算是对这批系列书籍的一个美好寄望。

　　雅思考试发展到今天,已经进入了一个相对稳定和成熟的时期;具体表现为考试内容范围逐渐固定,而考题形式进一步细化和多样化。比如口语和写作的话题范围已经几乎不再拓展,但问题的提问角度和文字表现形式却会推陈出新。再如听力和阅读的场景范围也已几乎囊括了国外日常生活与学习的主要方面,但其中所涉及的具体知识点却还有很多的资源可以利用。因此,就需要有这样的一种学术力量,它应该能够概括和把握雅思考试的总体特征,同时还要能够剖析考试中现有各种题型的具体特点,并且还要能够在此基础之上,提出行之有效的解决方案。

　　"低碳雅思"系列书籍,以历年雅思考试真题信息为基础,挑选和还原了一大批考试中曾经出现过的试题。这些试题反映了雅思考试的出题思路和能力考查重点,在题型设置上也囊括了所有雅思考试中所独有的特殊题型,对于正处于备考过程中的读者,或有计划参加雅思考试的读者,都有很强的指导作用。同时,书中还配有若干的专项训练和背景知识补充，能够为读者提供一个全方位的考试导航。

　　雅思考试在中国的盛行是与中国教育行业的高速发展不可分的，它为众多的中国学生提供了接受国际先进教育的机会。然而，因为中西教育传统的巨大差别，雅思对于很多学生来说并不是一道很容易迈过的门槛。作为教育行业的新来者，对雅思考试进行不断的深入研究，我们责无旁贷。"低碳雅思"是一个起点，在不久的将来，我们会为广大的读者提供更多更优秀的专业备考书籍。

纳思英语教研中心

2011.4.19

目　录

第一章　关于雅思口语

一、雅思口语考试简介

　　雅思考试口语部分通过考生与考官之间进行一对一交流的形式,考查考生日常会话、对熟悉话题作一定长度的描述以及与考官之间的互动能力。考试时间为 11—14 分钟,考试全程分为三个部分,考生需要在三个部分中使用不同的口语技能进行表达(雅思考试口语部分将被录音)。

　　口语考试三部分的具体流程如下:

部分	互动的内容	时间长度
1.	简介以及问答: 首先考官会核对考生身份,紧接着考生需要进行一个简单的自我介绍,随后考官会就考生所熟悉的话题进行提问。	4—5 分钟
2.	个人陈述: 考官将给考生一个答题任务卡,卡上有一个相关的话题。考生有一分钟的准备时间(如笔记),然后需就此话题进行 1 到 2 分钟的陈述。	3—4 分钟
3.	双向讨论: 考官将与考生就第二部分中出现的话题较为抽象的部分进行双向讨论。	4—5 分钟

请注意:

　　1) 在预定的口试时间前 30 分钟到达考试中心并签到。未能在考试前 15 分钟到达考试中心并签到的考生,将有可能被取消参加口试的资格,并不得转考、退考或退费。参加口试须带上身份证。

　　2) 听从工作人员的指挥,在候考室待考。工作人员会带领您到考试室。在考试室外等候考官请您进入。

　　3) 在完成口试后,立即离开考场。不要与任何人谈及您的考试情况,否则可能会被视作违反考场纪律。

二、雅思口语考试具体形式与内容

第一部分

1) 考试形式如何?

考官会让考生进行自我简介,并核对考生的身份。之后,考官会就考生熟悉的话题

（如朋友、兴趣习惯或者食物）进行询问。为保证题目的一致性，这些问题都是从一个事先拟定的范围内抽取的。

2）考试时间有多长？

这部分考试时间大约为4—5分钟。

3）这部分考查的是什么技能？

这部分考查的是考生就日常性的观点和信息、常见的生活经历或情形以回答问题的形式进行交流的能力。

第二部分

1）考试形式如何？

这部分内容为考生作个人陈述。考官会交给考生一个答题任务卡、铅笔和草稿纸做笔记。答题任务卡上会给出一个话题和需要在个人陈述中包含的要点，并且在最后提示考生解释这个话题的某一个方面。请注意，有效地使用答题任务卡上的提示可以有效地帮助考生思考讲述的话题、组织内容、并持续地陈述2分钟时间。在准备时间内做一些笔记也可以帮助考生安排好陈述的结构。考生会有1分钟的准备时间，之后考官会要求考生就相关的内容讲述1—2分钟。考官会在2分钟后打断考生，并在最后再提一两个问题作为结束语。

以下是一个第二部分的任务卡范例：

Describe a teacher who has greatly influenced you in your education.

You should say:

1. where you met him / her

2. what subject he / she taught

3. what was special about him / her

4. explain why this person influenced you so much.

You will have to talk about the topic for 1 to 2 minutes. You have one minute to think about what you are going to say. You can make some notes if you wish.

2）考试时间有多长？

这部分考试时间大约为3—4分钟。

3）这部分考查的是什么技能？

这部分考查的是考生（在没有任何其他提示的情况下）就一个特定的话题进行较长时间的陈述的能力，考查考生是否能恰当地运用语言、是否能连贯地组织自己的观点。考生有可能需要联系自己的经历来完成这部分内容。

第三部分

1）考试形式如何？

在这部分考试中，考官和考生将对第二部分中所涉及的话题进行讨论，讨论将会更加广泛和抽象，在恰当的时候还会更加深入。

2）考试时间有多长？

这部分考试时间大约为 4—5 分钟。

3）这部分考查的是什么技能？

这部分考查的是考生表达和论述看法、分析、讨论以及深入思考问题的能力。

第二章 雅思口语评分标准与对策解析

一、雅思考试评分体系简介

雅思考试的所有阅卷工作由经过训练的评分人员和考官在考试中心进行。评分人员受过专门训练,了解雅思评分相关政策,而且切实做到按照评分标准给听力和阅读考卷评分。每隔一年对评分人员进行测评,以确保评分符合标准。在每个考试中心,会进行系统化的监测,并对一定比例的答题纸实施双重阅卷。对于雅思写作和口语考官的招聘和培训按照既定标准进行。除了会持续监测考官的表现之外,还会每隔一年测评考官,以确保按照标准评分。

雅思考试采用国际认可的9分制评分系统,准确反映考生的语言水平。每个分数级别有对应的描述。总分可以是整数分或半分。九个分数段及其描述如下:

9分　专家水平

具有完全的英语运用能力,做到适当、精确、流利并能完全理解语言。

8分　优秀水平

能将英语运用自如,只是有零星的错误或用词不当。在不熟悉语境下可能出现误解,可将复杂细节的争论掌握得相当好。

7分　良好水平

能有效运用英语,虽然偶尔出现不准确、不适当和误解。大致可将复杂的英语掌握得不错,也能理解详细的推理。

6分　合格水平

大致能有效运用英语,虽然有不准确、不适当和误解发生,但能使用并理解比较复杂的英语,特别是在熟悉的语境下。

5分　基础水平

可部分运用英语,在大多数情况下可明白大致的意思。虽然经常出现错误,但在经常涉及的领域内可应付基本的沟通。

4分　有限水平

只限在熟悉的状况下有基本的理解力,在理解与表达上常发生问题,无法使用复杂英语。

3分　极有限水平

在极熟悉的情况下也只能进行一般的沟通,频繁发生沟通障碍。

2分　初学水平

除非在熟悉的语境下,几乎只能使用孤立单词或短句表达最基本的信息,不能达成有效沟通。难以听懂或者看懂英语。

1 分　不懂英语

最多能说出个别单词,根本无法用英语沟通。

0 分　考生缺席

缺乏评分依据。

请注意:

雅思考试的所有阅卷工作都由经过训练的评分人员和考官在考试中心进行。评分人员受过专门训练,了解雅思评分相关政策,而且切实做到按照评分标准给考卷评分。每隔一年对评分人员进行测评,以确保评分符合标准。在每个考试中心,会进行系统化的监测,并对一定比例的答题纸实施双重阅卷。对于雅思口语考官的招聘和培训按照既定标准进行。除了会持续监测考官的表现之外,还会每隔一年测评考官,以确保按照标准评分。

二、雅思口语考试评分标准

雅思考试口语部分的评分标准有四方面:
- 流畅性和结构层次
- 词汇来源
- 语法的多样性和准确性
- 语音

这四个方面在口语部分总分中所占的比重是完全相同的。并且从 2007 年 7 月 1 日开始,口语成绩有整分和半分之分。以下就是对口语考试评分标准四个方面的详细解释:

Fluency and coherence——流畅性和结构层次

这指的是考生能否使用正常水平的连贯性、语速,是否能够在观点的表达上和语言的使用上达到结构层次清晰、互相关联。

Lexical resource——词汇来源

这指的是考生使用的词汇量的范围、能否用这些词汇清晰地表达意思和态度,其中包括所使用的词汇是否多样、是否可以运用相关技巧绕过词汇障碍(如用不同方式表达相同的意思)。

Grammatical range and accuracy——语法的多样性和准确性

这指的是考生使用的语法结构的范围、能否正确和恰当地运用这些语法结构。在评分过程中,考生的表达的长度、复杂程度、以及语法错误对交流的影响等因素都在考查范围之内。

Pronunciation——语音

这指的是考生的表达是否可为他人理解、考生能否运用语音的内容表达意义。在评分过程中,考生在表达中造成理解障碍的次数、母语对英语表达的影响的次数都在考查范围之内。

三、雅思口语考试评分标准解析

所谓"对症下药":要获得有效的口语对策,首先要弄清楚的,就是口语考试9个分数段分别对应的能力要求;我们来看一下雅思分数段的官方描述:

• **Band 9**

Fluency and coherence	Speaks fluently with only rare repetition or self-correction; any hesitation is content-related rather than to find words or grammar. Speaks coherently with fully appropriate cohesive features. Develops topics fully and appropriately.
Lexical resource	Uses vocabulary with full flexibility and precision in all topics. Uses idiomatic language naturally and accurately.
Grammatical range and accuracy	Uses a full range of structures naturally and appropriately. Produces consistently accurate structures apart from "slips" characteristic of native speaker speech.
Pronunciation	Uses a full range of pronunciation features with precision and subtlety. Sustains flexible use of features throughout. Is effortless to understand.

解释:9分的"专家水平"其实指的就是说出地道的"本国人"表达,即与英国人、美国人、澳大利亚人等以英语为母语的人们平常所做的表达无异。达到这个水准,需要具备:

1)表达流利,仅有极少量的重复与自我更正(with only rare repetition or self-correction);同时任何表达中的犹豫都只能是因为在回答过程中对回答内容的思考,而不能是因为在寻找合适的词汇与语法结构(hesitation is content-related rather than to find words or grammar);表达中需要有合适的连接性内容来保持内容的连贯性(coherently with fully appropriate cohesive features);能充分地拓展话题(Develops topics fully and appropriately)。

2)词汇的使用手段要多样和精确(full flexibility and precision),并且最好能自然和正确地使用"习语"表达(idiomatic language)。

3)语法结构的使用要多样且合理(use a full range of structures naturally and appropriately),可以有少量"本国人"在做口语表达时偶尔会有的错误("slips" characteristic of native speaker speech)。

4)发音要准确和到位,体现多种发音特点(a full range of pronunciation features),且做到灵活多变(flexible),所做表达能让听者毫不费力地听懂(effortless to understand)。

• **Band 8**

Fluency and coherence	Speaks fluently with only occasional repetition or self-correction; hesitation is usually content-related and only rarely to search for language. Develops topics coherently and appropriately.
Lexical resource	Uses a wide vocabulary resource readily and flexibly to convey precise meaning. Uses less common and idiomatic vocabulary skillfully, with occasional inaccuracies. Uses paraphrase effectively as required.
Grammatical range and accuracy	Uses a wide range of structures flexibly. Produces a majority of error-free sentences with only very occasional inappropriacies or basic / non-systematic errors.
Pronunciation	Uses a wide range of pronunciation features. Sustains flexible use of features, with only occasional lapses. Is easy to understand throughout; non-native accent has minimal effect on intelligibility.

解释:8分属于优秀水平。8分水平的表达虽然仍能见到一些"非母语"表达者的痕迹,但是尚可以和考官进行自如顺畅的交流,几乎没有大的障碍。达到这个水准,需要具备:

1）表达流利,有偶尔的重复与自我更正（with only occasional repetition or self-correction）;同时表达中的犹豫大都是因为在回答过程中对回答内容的思考,只有少量是因为在寻找合适的辞藻（hesitation is usually content-related and only rarely to search for language）;能合理拓展话题,并做出连贯的表达（develops topics coherently and appropriately）。

2）词汇的使用能体现出广度和精确度（a wide vocabulary resource readily and flexibly to convey precise meaning）;能使用一些非常见表达和"习语",并允许存在少量不精确之处（uses less common and idiomatic vocabulary skillfully, with occasional inaccuracies）;能够在表达中体现同意转换的能力（uses paraphrase effectively）。

3）语法结构的使用要灵活（flexibly）;表达中绝大部分的句子都是没有错误的（a majority of error-free sentences）,但可有少量的表达不合理之处（only very occasional inappropriacies or basic / non-systematic errors）。

4）发音要体现多种发音特点（a wide range of pronunciation features）,且只存在少量偏差（occasional lapses）;所做表达能让听者很容易地听懂,即使有母语发音的痕迹也不会影响理解（minimal effect on intelligibility）。

• **Band 7**

Fluency and coherence	Speaks at length without noticeable effort or loss of coherence. May demonstrate language-related hesitation at times, or some repetition and / or self-correction. Uses a range of connectives and discourse markers but not always appropriately.
Lexical resource	Uses vocabulary resource flexibly to discuss a variety of topics. Uses some less common and idiomatic vocabulary and shows some awareness of style and collocation, with some inappropriate choices. Uses paraphrase effectively.
Grammatical range and accuracy	Uses a range of complex structures with some flexibility. Frequently produces error-free sentences, though some grammatical mistakes persist.
Pronunciation	Shows all the positive features of Band 6 and some, but not all, of the positive features of Band 8.

解释:7分属于良好水平。通常7分水平的表达能够明显地让人感觉到是来自于"非母语"语言使用者的,但是对于英语习得者来说,是一个相当不错的表现。达到这个水准,需要具备:

1) 能够不太费力地使表达达到一定篇幅,且没有明显的连贯性上的缺陷(at length without noticeable effort or loss of coherence);可能存在一些因为找不到合适辞藻的犹豫,并且可能伴随一些重复和自我更正(language-related hesitation at times, or some repetition and / or self-correction);表达中包含多样的连接性内容(a range of connectives and discourse markers),但不一定都能够正确地使用(not always appropriately)。

2) 词汇的使用能体现出灵活性(Uses vocabulary resource flexibly);能使用一些非常见表达和"习语"(less common and idiomatic vocabulary),能够注意到在表达风格和搭配上讲究(awareness of style and collocation),可能存在少量不精确之处(inappropriate choices);能够在表达中体现同意转换的能力(uses paraphrase effectively)。

3) 能够灵活地使用各种复杂的语法结构(frequently produces error-free sentences);能够使用大量的没有错误的句子来进行表达(a majority of error-free sentences),但可有少量的语法错误(some grammatical mistakes)。

4) 发音上含有所有6分水平的积极因素,和一些8分水平的积极因素。

• **Band 6**

Fluency and coherence	Is willing to speak at length, though may lose coherence at times due to occasional repetition, self-correction or hesitation. Uses a range of connectives and discourse markers but not always appropriately.

Lexical resource	Has a wide enough vocabulary to discuss topics at length and make meaning clear in spite of inappropriacies. Generally paraphrases successfully.
Grammatical range and accuracy	Uses a mix of simple and complex structures, but with limited flexibility. May make frequent mistakes with complex structures, though these rarely cause comprehension problems.
Pronunciation	Uses a range of pronunciation features with mixed control. Shows some effective use of features but this is not sustained. Can generally be understood throughout, though mispronunciation of individual words or sounds reduces clarity at times.

解释:6分属于及格水平。达到这个水平的语言使用者能够基本满足在英美等国日常生活和学习中的语言需求。达到这个水准的表达,通常具有以下特点:

1) 能够主动给出达到一定篇幅的表达(willing to speak at length),可能会时不时地因为重复,自我更正或犹豫影响到表达的连贯性(lose coherence);表达中包含一定的连接性内容(a range of connectives and discourse markers),但不一定都能够正确地使用(not always appropriately)。

2) 能够有足够多的词汇量来满足表达的需要(wide enough vocabulary);存在不合适的表达但不影响清晰度(make meaning clear in spite of inappropriacies);总体而言能够进行一定的同义转换(generally paraphrases successfully)。

3) 能够搭配使用简单和复杂的语法结构(a mix of simple and complex structures),但缺乏灵活度(limited flexibility);在使用复杂结构的时候会出现频繁的错误(frequent mistakes with complex structures,),虽然这些错误几乎不影响理解(rarely cause comprehension problems)。

4) 语音上存在混搭现象(a range of pronunciation features with mixed control);能有效地使用一些语音技巧(some effective use),但不能一直保持(not sustained);总体而言能够让人理解,但个别发音错误会降低表达的清晰度(mispronunciation of individual words or sounds reduces clarity at times)。

• Band 5

Fluency and coherence	Usually maintains flow of speech but uses repetition, self-correction and / or slow speech to keep going. May over use certain connectives and discourse markers. Produces simple speech fluently, but more complex communication causes fluency problems.
Lexical resource	Manages to talk about familiar and unfamiliar topics but uses vocabulary with limited flexibility. Attempts to use paraphrase but with mixed success.

Grammatical range and accuracy	Produces basic sentence forms with reasonable accuracy. Uses a limited range of more complex structures，but these usually contain errors and may cause some comprehension problems.
Pronunciation	Shows all the positive features of Band 4 and some，but not all，of the positive features of Band 6.

解释：5分属于基础水平。达到这个水平的语言使用者能够勉强满足在英美等国日常生活和学习中的语言需求。处于这个水准的表达，通常具有以下特点：

1）能保持语流的进行（usually maintains flow of speech），但是存在重复、自我更正和过慢语速等现象；会过多使用某些连接信息（over use certain connectives and discourse markers）；能流利地使用简单语言（simple speech fluently），但在使用复杂表达时经常犯错（more complex communication causes fluency problems）。

2）表达时词汇的使用缺乏灵活性（uses vocabulary with limited flexibility）；会尝试进行同义转换，但是往往不成功（Attempts to use paraphrase but with mixed success）。

3）在使用简单句型时尚可保持一定的准确性（basic sentence forms with reasonable accuracy），但对于复杂句型的储备不足（a limited range of more complex structures），并且使用时会出现错误，从而造成理解上的难度（contain errors and may cause some comprehension problems）。

4）发音上含有所有4分水平的积极因素，和一些6分水平的积极因素。

• **Band 4**

Fluency and coherence	Cannot respond without noticeable pauses and may speak slowly, with frequent repetition and self-correction. Links basic sentences but with repetitious use of simple connectives and some breakdowns in coherence.
Lexical resource	Is able to talk about familiar topics but can only convey basic meaning on unfamiliar topics and makes frequent errors in word choice. Rarely attempts paraphrase.
Grammatical range and accuracy	Produces basic sentence forms and some correct simple sentences but subordinate structures are rare. Errors are frequent and may lead to misunderstanding.
Pronunciation	Uses a limited range of pronunciation features. Attempts to control features but lapses are frequent. Mispronunciations are frequent and cause some difficulty for the listener.

解释：4分属于有限水平。处于这个水平的语言使用者无法满足到英美等国的语言需求，但通过一定阶段有效的学习后，可以满足一些生活和学习方面的基本需求。处于这个水准的表达，通常具有以下特点：

1）无法流畅地进行表达，有明显的停顿（pauses）和语速过慢的现象（speak

slowly），且有频繁的重复和自我更正（frequent repetition and self-correction）；能对句子进行必要的连接（links basic sentences），但会过多地使用一些简单的连接信息破坏表达的连贯性（repetitious use of simple connectives and some breakdowns in coherence）。

2）能应付熟悉的话题，但对于不熟悉的话题只能做出含糊的表达，并且会存在频繁的用词错误（frequent errors in word choice）；几乎不会使用同义转换（rarely attempts paraphrase）。

3）能使用基本句型和一些简单句型，很少使用从句（subordinate structures are rare）；错误频出，影响理解（misunderstanding）。

4）只掌握有限的发音特征（a limited range of pronunciation features）；尝试去控制语音但经常出现失误（attempts to control features but lapses are frequent），因此造成理解上的困难（cause some difficulty for the listener）。

• **Band 3**

Fluency and coherence	Speaks with long pause. Has limited ability to link simple sentences. Gives only simple responses and is frequently unable to convey basic message.
Lexical resource	Uses simple vocabulary to convey personal information. Has insufficient vocabulary for less familiar topics.
Grammatical range and accuracy	Attempts basic sentence forms but with limited success, or relies on apparently memorised utterances. Makes numerous errors except in memorised expressions.
Pronunciation	Shows some of the features of Band 2 and some, but not all, of the positive features of Band 4.

解释：3分属于极有限水平。处于这个水平的语言使用者暂且不具备到英美等国学习和生活的能力，需进行长时间的学习。处于这个水准的表达，通常具有以下特点：

1）表达中会有很长的停顿（speaks with long pause）；连接句子的能力很有限（limited ability to link simple sentences）；只能给出简单回复，经常无法传递基本信息（frequently unable to convey basic message）。

2）会使用简单的词汇表达个人信息（use simple vocabulary to convey personal information），但应对不熟悉的话题，所具备的词汇量不足（insufficient vocabulary for less familiar topics）。

3）尝试使用简单的句型但是成功率有限（limited success），或所作回答主要基于背诵来的信息（relies on apparently memorised utterances）；除了背诵的信息，回答中存在相当多的错误（numerous errors）。

4）发音上含有所有2分水平的因素，和一些4分水平中的积极因素。

• Band 2

Fluency and coherence	Pauses lengthily before most words. Little communication possible.
Lexical resource	Only produces isolated words or memorised utterances.
Grammatical range and accuracy	Cannot produce basic sentence forms.
Pronunciation	Speech is often unintelligible.

解释:2分属于初学水平。处于这个水平的语言使用者完全不具备到英美等国学习和生活的能力,需进行系统性的学习。处于这个水准的表达,通常具有以下特点:

1)在说出大部分单词前都会有长时间的停顿(pauses lengthily before most words);很难有交流的可能(little communication possible)。

2)只能说出个别的单词(isolated words),或者背诵信息(memorised utterances)。

3)在表达中无法使用简单句型(cannot produce basic sentence forms)。

4)发音经常让人无法理解(often unintelligible)。

• Band 1

No communication possible; no rateable language.

解释:取得1分成绩的人被定义为"不懂英语"。处于这个水准的考生,被考官认为是无法交流的。

• Band 0

Does not attend.

解释:0分只会在考生缺考的情况下给出。

四、雅思口语考试备考策略

现在根据上面一节对雅思口语考试评分标准的解析,提出下面3个建议:

如何步入5.5—6.5分的区间

一般来说,6.5,6分和5.5分是大部分英美院校的分别对于研究生课程,本科生课程和大学预科课程的分数要求。要到达这个分数区间的备考策略如下所示:

1)掌握常用语法。如时态、主谓一致、主被动语态等基本的语法知识,可帮助考生在作答时不犯语法错误,保证语言表达的基本正确,让考官能够较清晰地明确考生想要表达的意思。

2)掌握常用话题词汇,并且在此基础上就各个话题进行广泛的构思训练。常用的话题词汇如兴趣爱好话题的词汇、旅游话题的词汇等,首先可以保证考生有可用来会话的基本素材,不会在考场上词穷;而在此基础上的构思训练可以让考生在考场上作出熟练地回答,减少回答中的停顿和犹豫。备考者在做构思训练的过程中,最好能够将一些关键句词用英语进行记录,有助于在考场上表达关键信息时脱口而出。

3）掌握一些简单但很实用的表达套路。一些口语表达中常用的套路如 a huge fan of something, has to do with, is about to 等,可以帮助考生在进行口语表达时,快速准确地进行表达。而且由于这些概念在日常表达中都属于高频表达,有利于考官对考生表述的清晰理解。

4）更多地使用逻辑连接词／短语。逻辑连接词如 because, however, on the one hand, on the other hand 等本身非常简单,但在表达中合理的运用却可以使得句子与句子之间连接变得流畅,从而向听者非常清晰地梳理出表达中的逻辑,而逻辑是人类理解事物的主线,一个简洁明了的逻辑是清晰理解的重点所在。

5）掌握正确的词汇发音,尤其是重读落在哪个音节,单词中长短元音的区分,一些辅音正确的发音位置等。词汇的正确发音是表达能让人理解的基础。

如何步入 6.5—7.5 分的区间

6.5—7.5 的分数可以大大的帮助留学生进入英美国家排名靠前的大学,并且达到这个水准的学生就具备了积极参与国外生活中的聊天对话和学习中的课堂讨论的语言基础。

1）在掌握常用语法的基础上,学会一些简洁的修辞方法。平时进行口语表达练习时,有意识地使用一些可以使会话内容增色的修辞结构,如"形容词＋名词(a terrible memory)"、"副词＋形容词(fairly easy)"、"副词＋动词(quickly find)"、"介词短语(out of control)"等。这样可以让口语表述具有立体感,从简单的陈述变成精彩的描述。

2）在自己的词汇库里适量增加一些"准专业词汇"——貌似有一定专业性,但不会专业到常人听不懂,如 iPhone application, artificial intelligence, indie music 等,此外,还要对各个常见话题进行深入的思考,不满足于没有新意的泛泛之谈,产生属于自己的观点。这样做可以使得回答更具个性化,能让考官对你有一个深入的印象,成为 the one 而不是 one of the many,让自己的大脑具备 personality 和 sensitivity。

3）掌握使用一些有效果的表达套路。一些很具效果的表达,往往从语言角度而言是难度比较大的,但我们可以通过记住一些固定的套路,来降低表达的难度,让自己在考场上也能做出不同凡响的口头表达。如 the fact ... doesn't mean ..., e.g. The fact it is changed doesn't mean that is has improved. The fact we're different from others doesn't necessarily mean that we're wrong. 又如 It is ... not ... that matters, e.g. It is quality not quantity that matters. It is personality not nationality that matters.

4）在掌握常用连接词的基础之上,对口语表达进行更好的结构梳理,养成先想后说的习惯,即作答前先在心里草拟一个作答提纲,可以是总分总,也可以是总分,也可以是分总,还可以细节到某个关键点大概要举哪些例子,进行哪些理论。这样可以使整体的作答更加有条理,更加清晰。

5）掌握一些常速语篇中的发音特征,如连读、略读、吞音、变音等,以使自己会话的语篇不但做到发音正确,而且吐字流畅、悦耳、不勉强。

如何步入 7.5 分以上的区间

获得 7.5 分以上考生在选择申请大学的时候,对于大部分院校的大部分专业来说,已经没有任何语言分数上的限制了。而且这个口语水平也基本保证了学生能够在课堂讨论和生活会话中自如地进行自我表达。

1) 在掌握基础语法,能熟练使用常用修辞手法的基础上,再试着去掌握一些高难度的修辞方法,如同位语 It is Roan, his brother, that introduced me to my partner. 后置定语 A book that discusses some of the most challenging topics. 等。这样一来就可以达到评分标准里所说的(demonstrate full / a wide range of grammatical structures)。

2) 学会对口语话题进行透彻的思考,发挥抽象思维,对话题和所涉及到的现象进行追本溯源的分析,以帮助我们的回答能够足够客观,足够成熟,足够有说服性。

3) 试着去使用一些英语中的俗语,如 He is only chewing fats. Jackie is a real bottler! 等,来使自己的表达变得更加地道。同时可以适当去收集名人名言,然后合适地进行使用;可以从最简单的开始,如 Knowledge is power, as is said by Francis Bacon.

4) 在作答时避免自说自话,学会用沟通和交流的方法进行会话;语言使用的最高境界关注的已经不是语言本身,而是语言之外的东西,如通过语言所投射出来的思想和态度。

5) 学会去区分几种不同的口音,如美国的新英格兰口音、英国的河口口音等,并且按照自身情况,选择口音;在口语表达中,最好做到口音的一致,不要"英美澳"混杂。

第三章 雅思口语发音突破

一、八种迅速改变英语发音的方法

方法一：两秒钟练习法

长元音和双元音的发音要超过两秒钟。现在就尝试，你的英语马上悦耳动听，充满自信。

I am crazy about Chinese food.

【发音分析：这个句子里面有 6 个长元音和双元音！这六个音几乎占了 12 秒】

I'd like to buy a bicycle for my sister.

【发音分析：这个句子包含了 5 个超级饱满大嘴/aɪ/音】

方法二：收小腹练习法

这是一个神奇的练习法，可以让你的英语瞬间变得地道。中国式的英语的最大问题在于底气不足，拖泥带水。"收小腹练习法"可以立刻改变这种状况。此方法仅针对短元音。

Difficult　　This question is very difficult.

Pretty　　Your English is pretty good.

Minute　　Please wait a minute.

Develop　　China is a developing country.

方法三：大嘴练习法

想要说好英语，就必须想办法把嘴巴和口腔撑开，加大，扩充。英语中有几个超级大嘴音，比如说/aɪ/，/aʊ/，/ɒ/。下面让我们集中操练。

1) 超级饱满双元音：/aɪ/

Would you like some ice cream?

My flight leaves at nine thirty-five.

I will fly to China tonight.

2) 鬼哭狼嚎音：/aʊ/

There is no doubt about it.

I found a mouse in my house last night.

Open your mouth and pronounce the sound loudly.

3) 感叹祖国美好山河音：/ɒ/

This is an impossible goal.

Please give me your honest opinion. What do you think?

She is not very popular in our school.

方法四:咬嘴唇集中练习法

中文里有/f/音,但是没有/v/这个音,于是这就导致了中国人发音的另外一个巨大的困难。正确地区分发音/v/和/w/。为了表示你征服这个发音的决心,每次发这个音时,都请你故意使劲咬住你的下嘴唇,像是很愤怒的样子。

I really need a long vacation.

That's a beautiful view.

I am very tired.

Please forgive me.

Leave me alone.

I have to save money for my future.

Have a nice trip.

It's over.

方法五:三大鼻音练习法

鼻音是中国人发音的另外一大难点。因为中文里很少有以鼻音结尾的字,而英语中到处都是以"三大鼻音"结尾的单词。

1) 闭嘴鼻音:/m/

sometimes:有时候

Sometimes I make my mom very <u>mad at</u> me.

2) 开口鼻音:/n/

nine:九

Jim bought his girlfriend nine hundred and ninety-nine roses for her birthday.

3) 后鼻音:/ŋ/

interesting:有趣的

Learning English with Jason is interesting.

方法六:连读练习法

如果一个单词的结尾是辅音,后一个单词的开头是元音,在实际朗读的过程中就会把它们连读起来,这种现象就叫连读。

I'm loving it!

How's everything?

Take it easy.

Please get out of my house.

方法七:失爆练习法

两个爆破音相邻,第一个爆破音只形成阻碍。常见的爆破音有/k/, /g/, /t/, /d/, /p/, /b/等等。

See you in Sep-tember.

Good-bye.

Good morning.

This is a good-chance. You should-catch it.

Please take-good-care of my dog.

Stop-talking. Listen to me.

方法八: 家用7步训练法

训练法一:背"新概念"

Memorizing articles and vocabularies from *New Concept English* books is an excellent method to build up the basic foundation of a student. New concept one almost has 1,000 vocabularies and is suitable for primary or middle school students. New concept two has 2,500 to 3,000 vocabularies. A student will have at least collected 4,000 words after finishing studying these two books and it is already adequate to have a band score of 6 in IELTS oral English.

训练法二:找一些自己感兴趣的听力材料

Search for materials that you will be interested in such as comics and magazines. Students can try to read aloud the content to practice their oral English. The sentences and vocabularies in these materials can be straightly used if a student would like to express similar idea or thinking of the same topic.

训练法三:看美国电影

Imitating how actors and actress deliver their lines in a movie is surely a good way to improve a student's oral English. The scenes in the movie will allow students to know or guess what the actor / actress wants to relay. Plus, the students will not only learn how to say the sentences they learned from the movie but also the right expressions and intonations of them as well.

训练法四:跟外国朋友交流

Get an English-speaking friend and then communicate to him / her as much as you can. Make sure they're nice enough to repeat what they say if you do not understand them. Try to invite them to play basketball, baseball or whatever sports both of you are interested in. Make them part of your everyday life. If you talk to them a lot, it will really improve your listening and speaking skills.

训练法五:熟悉固定句子结构和句型

Students should familiarize themselves with the basic structures of sentences such as 1.主语——动词——表语.2.主语——动词.3.主语——动词——宾语.4.主语——动

词——宾语——宾语. 5. 主语——动词——宾语——补语. On the other hand, phrases like: enjoy doing sth, be fond of doing sth, feel like doing sth, be busy doing / with sth, carry sth with sb, see sb do / doing sth, hear sb do / doing sth, like doing / to do sth, would rather do sth should also be memorised to be able to improve the student's oral English.

训练法六:创造一个英语环境

Try to find some partners to practice your oral English. For example, your friends or classmates that are also interested in improving their speaking ability. If a student is having a difficulty to find one, English corner is a suitable place as it is where they can exchange English study experience, widen their sights and improve interest in English. If it's not easy to get English partners or having little chance to attend an English corner, then we have to create an English environment ourselves by speaking English to ourselves. For instance, you can talk to yourself about what you have seen or what you have done. This may sound crazy but it worked for a large amount of students.

训练法七:听广播

When listening to radio, students can review a lot of English usage such as vocabulary, grammatical structures, intonation and accent. Furthermore, they can learn new words and expressions by hearing them frequently in the radio. And general knowledge from news, features, or even advertising spots are certainly beneficial for regular listeners. And also, listening to radio can be a good "hobby" while students do other things such as cooking, ironing, exercising, relaxing, etc.

二、十个口语练习小贴士

1) Listen to yourself.

如果你听不到自己的发音问题,要纠正就很难了。试着把你讲的话录下来并和英语为母语的人士讲的对比一下。应对雅思口语非常有效。

2) Slow down!

很多英语学习者常说语速太快容易养成他们的坏习惯。由于太快而模糊不清是口语考试的大忌。所以我们要 accuracy 然后才是 fluency,每天以单音节开始操练一些基本语言,然后练单词,再把几个词连在一起,组成句子。这样你就能慢慢开始表达自己的思想了。

3) Picture it …

闭上你的眼睛并在说出口之前想一想如何发这个音。想象出口型和脸部动作。这个可以配合看电影来做,留意 Hollywood 的明星是怎么样一字一句地说出那些令人神魂颠倒的话语的。

4) Get physical!

发音是个形体动作。要学会嘴巴的发声方法和移动肌肉的方式。每天集中训练几个音。你发 this，thank，they 和 little，wool 等单词困难吗？试试发"th"，将你的舌头放在齿间（不要咬住）并从口中吐气。感受气流从你的舌间吹过。

5) Watch yourself.

站在镜子前查看当你发某些固定音时的嘴型、唇型和舌头的位置。和你看到的 native speaker 的发音对比！平时还可以把自己的发音模样录成 video，仔细观察比较。

6) Copy the experts.

绝对没有取代从专家——英语母语人士处学习发音的方式。因此仔细听！听英语广播节目并看英语的电视节目和电影。尽量不要念字幕！模仿你所听到的——就算你还不肯定他们说的话。

7) Practice makes perfect.

发音的问题迟迟不能解决就是因为我们害怕犯错。想象一些场景：第一次见面、在饭店点菜、询问方向，然后你自己表演出对话内容。别害羞！

8) Find a language buddy.

从其他人处获得反馈是非常重要的。找一个对提高英语水平同样感兴趣的朋友。试着更换录音资料这样你就可以互相听对方的发音。记住录完要重新听听，找出错误和闪光点啊。

9) Be poetic.

好的发音不仅是掌握单独的音节，还是对 intonation（声音的升降调）和 stress（对单词中一些音节和句子中的一些单词更大声更清晰的发音）的理解。大声念一些诗歌、演讲、歌曲，集中练习单词的重音和音调。

10) Sing a song!

学习一些英语流行歌曲的歌词并跟着唱。唱歌帮助你放松并能让这些词说出来，同时帮助改进你的语音和语调。

第四章 雅思口语第一部分—— 一般问题

一、最初开场时的几个相关问题

在进入考场后,考生会被问到这几个问题:

1) Can I see your identification / identification card, please?

解析:这个问题出现在 check your identity 部分。考生只需简单回答 yes,随即将自己的 ID card 递给考官就好。

2) What's your name?

解析:在开场考官询问名字,考生只要给出自己的名字就好。注意,是中文全名。不要直接报英文名字。因为这个部分还是属于 check your identity。

例子:Well, my full name is ×××, and you can call me John / Jane, that's my English name.

My name is ×××, and my English name is John / Jane. You're welcome to call me John / Jane.

注意:Avoid saying "my Chinese name is ..."对我们中国人来说,其实最初是没有中文名字和英文名字之分的。只需要说 full name 即可。

二、第一部分话题归总

在这个部分,考生会遇到各种各样的贴近考生生活的话题。答题主要原则如下:

T:topic sentence(开场句)

S:supporting details (支持细节)

C:conclusion(结论)

这个原则类似我们中文写作的一个总分总结构,以下一个例子就是根据总—分—总结构进行的作答:

Well, yes, I do like music. (Topic Sentence)

I started to listen to some pop music when I was in junior high school and recently I'm quite into rock music for the fact that rock music can cheer me up whenever I feel downright sad. I also want to try some jazz because one of my best friends recommend several very good jazz music to me. (Supporting Details)

So, basically, pop, rock and jazz are the music types that I like to listen. (Conclusion)

以下,根据以往考试的实际情况,我们把第一部分的话题概括为七大类,即工作、家庭、教育、考生、生活、兴趣和科技：

1）关于工作

Q：Are you a student or do you work?

A：Well，I'm a student currently majoring in English in a local university in Hangzhou. / I wish I were still a student. I just graduated from university six months ago and now I'm a math teacher in a high school.

Q：What job do you do? / Where do you work? / What do you do for a living? / What are some of your main responsibilities?

A：I'm working as an English teacher in a language training school. Basically，my job is trying to help those students who are struggling to get a decent score in IELTS and other tasks.

Q：Why did you choose this job?

A：Well，the main reason that I chose this job is that I want to make a difference. I like sharing my study experience with today's young people and hope that it can help them make right and good decisions about everything.

Q：How long have you been working?

A：I just graduated from college a year ago and spent a half on job hunting. So I've been working for only six months.

Q：Do you like the job?

A：Well，I think I like what I'm doing now. Being a teacher makes myself useful though sometimes I do feel exhausted.

A：Em，I'm not sure. I'm still trying to prove that it's possible to develop it as my career not just a job. You know，doing education is not easy everywhere. I need more time to adjust myself.

Q：Would you say it's an easy job?

A：Oh，it's definitely a difficult job. Every day I have to face different students with various previous learning experience. Selecting an appropriate teaching method became an essential part in my job.

Q：Have you received any training at work?

A：Yes，sure. We have many training sessions during work. For example，last week we had a training on how to engage students more effectively and as far as I know，we are going to have another similar session next month.

Q：Are you planning to change your job?

A：No，currently all I want to do is to focus on my students and do my best to help them learn more. I haven't thought about changing my job.

其他类似题目：
- In the future, what changes do you think will take place in the typical workplace?
- Would you like to receive some training (in the future)?
- What's the most difficult part of your job?
- Do you remember your first day at work?
- Do you need to work with other people at work?
- Do you prefer your life now, as a working person, to the life you had as a student?
- Would you recommend this job to other people?
- Do you think your university education prepared you well for the work you are doing now?

2) 关于家庭

Q: Where do you come from? / Where is your hometown?

A: I'm from a small town near Hangzhou named A. It is located in the west of Zhejiang Province and takes you around 1 hour drive from Hangzhou to my hometown.

Q: How long have you been living there / here?

A: I was born there, and never been to other cities for studying or living. So I've stayed in my hometown for over 20 years.

Q: Are there any scenic spots in your hometown?

A: Well, in fact, my hometown is very famous for its stunning sceneries. One of the most popular spots is ... lake which attracts lots of people from the whole nation.

Q: What tourist attractions are there in your hometown?

A: Well, being the capital city of Zhejiang Province, Hangzhou has a rich heritage and has become an important national tourist city with its stunning scenery. The West Lake, Linying Temple and Leifeng Pagoda attract thousands of people from the world every year.

Q: How has your hometown changed, compared to the past?

A: I think the biggest change is the traffic situation. In the past, there was no traffic jam at all. Nowadays, however, more and more cars came to my hometown and the traffic problem is getting more serious.

Q: Can you tell me something about your hometown?

A: Sure. My hometown has enjoyed a long history of over 2,000 years since Qin Dynasty. It was one of the seven ancient capitals of China. The profound cultural heritage in my hometown promotes the developments of Hangzhou's economy. Also，it has been reputed as the Land of Plenty and the Home of Silk for the fact that Hangzhou is famous for its abundant natural resources such as fish，rice and silk.

Q：What are the people like in your hometown?

A：There are always many different kinds of people everywhere. In my hometown people are mostly very simple，friendly and hospitable but a little conservative. If you visit my hometown and somehow get lost，just ask someone for directions，they will always be very helpful.

Q：What's famous about your hometown? / Is your hometown famous for anything?

A：Well，I am not sure what my hometown is really famous for. But a lot of people like the local food there like Crab Baozi，Shrimp Dumplings and many other seafood. Therefore，I guess my hometown is at least famous for its local snacks.

Q：Is there anything you don't like about your hometown?

A：Well，the first thing that jumps into my mind is the traffic jam and air pollution. Life can't be easy if you live in a city like this.

Q：What do you think needs to change in your hometown? / What do you think needs to be done to make your hometown a better place to live in? / If you could change one thing about your hometown，what would it be?

A：With the support from the people of my hometown，I would like to open more schools or even a college in my hometown because the present schools are already overcrowded with an average size for each class at over 50 students. So to ensure each student in my hometown receives a quality education，quick action must be taken to open more schools.

其他类似题目：

• What kind of activities do the people in your hometown would do in their spare time?

• Would you say your hometown is suitable for children to grow up in?

• Do you like your hometown? (Why? / Why not?)

• What sorts of buildings are there in your hometown?

• What's the weather usually like in your hometown?

• Has the weather in your hometown changed much in recent years?

3）关于教育

Q：How long have you studied English?

A：Well，I guess it's too long to remember. It seems that I started to learn English since I went to school. Maybe more than 15 years, I guess.

Q: What's your major?

A: I'm studying English in a local university. The main reason is I'm naturally good at it and I like it. I think learning language is like exploring another world. Plus, it's not difficult to find a decent job after I graduate from university.

A: I major in Business management and I find business is a wonderful world to explore. I am studying hard and hopefully one day I'll become a successful businessman.

Q: Why did you choose your major / Why did you choose ... as your major?

A: Well. The reasons that I chose Business as my majors are various. Firstly, I had an interest in Business since I was in junior high school. Secondly, my parents encouraged me to choose this major because people studying Business get higher salaries at work compared to others.

Q: Is your major important for your city / country?

A: I'm not sure. You know, China is a big country and people's definitions of importance differ from regions. According to the people around me, my major is not that important as others such as Economics or Finance. Not many students would like to study Philosophy nowadays.

Q: Do you like your major?

A: Well, I would say yes because my major has already became a part of my life. I'm used to it and will continue to live with it.

其他类似题目:
- Do you think it's important to choose a subject you like?
- What's the most useful / difficult part of your major?
- What subject(s) are you studying?
- What's the most interesting part of your course (your subject)?
- Are there any particular skills that you learn in your studies?
- How is your school (or university)?
- Could you say something about your university?
- Why are you taking the IELTS test?
- What are your future study plans?
- What are your future work plans (after you graduate)?
- When you start working, do you think you will prefer that to being a student?

4) 关于考生

Q: What's your name? / Can I have your name, please?

A：My full name is . . . and my English name is . . . You can call me . . .

Q：Who gave you this name?

A：My father. My mom told me that 24 years ago，before I was born，my father did lots of work on my name. He consulted several local scholars and checked several dictionaries and finally my name came out.

Q：Does your name have any special meaning?

A：Yes，my name does have some special meaning. As I said before，. . . is my family name and . . . is my given name. In China，. . . means / represents / stands for . . .

Q：Do you want to change your name?

A：No，I don't plan to. My name contains my parents' great love and their high expectations on me. I won't change it for any reasons.

5）关于生活

Q：What time do you usually get up?

A：It depends. I usually get up at 7 in the morning if I have class to go. But on weekends，I always stay with my bed until my mom comes to my room，yelling at me.

Q：What's your favourite time of (or，part of) the day?

A：It should be evenings. After a long day，I can do whatever I want to do to relax myself in the evening. For example，watching a movie with my boyfriend or hanging out with my close friends.

Q：How is your life today different to what it was when you were a child?

A：Well，the biggest difference should be the focus of my life. In the past，my life was fully occupied by study but now，I have more time to think about my future and choose a job，working it as my career.

Q：If you could change one thing about your daily routine，what would it be?

A：I'm currently happy with my daily routine. I don't think there is something need to be changed.

A：Well，if I could change one thing about my daily routine，I wish that I had more time to sleep. It seems that I never got enough sleep since I started to work as a lawyer.

Q：Where do you usually buy clothes?

A：Honestly，I'm not a fan for shopping. If I have to buy clothes，I prefer to do it online. It's more convenient and the price usually cheaper than some big shopping malls.

Q：Where do you think you can buy the most fashionable clothes?

A：Well，I'm not a person that always follows the latest fashion news. Thus，I've no idea about the places that can buy the most fashionable clothes. But I guess，maybe in some big shopping malls or online.

Q：What do you usually do when you have holidays?

A：Depends on my mood. If I'm happy，I probably will go to watch a movie or hold a party with my friends. If I feel upset，the only thing I would like to do in my holidays is to sleep，trying to forget everything.

Q：Would you like to go to the seaside for a holiday?

A：Sure. I love the sea. I believe that the sea has the power to make people feel peaceful.

A：Well，I'm fine with the seaside but the place that I would like to spend my holiday is some modern cities such as Hong Kong，New York or London.

Q：Why do you think people who don't live near the ocean like going to the seaside for a holiday?

A：I don't know about other people but personally speaking，the ocean can make me feel relaxed and take my mind off from my busy study life. So，maybe that is also the reason why people like to choose the ocean for a holiday.

Q：How often do you usually surf the Internet?

A：To be honest，I surf the Internet every day. I can't imagine how I am gonna survive without it. It is actually a part of my life.

Q：Do you often chat with strangers on MSN or in other chatting rooms?

A：No，I mean，I wouldn't talk with someone I don't even know，you know，that is pointless / meaningless，and the most important reason is the internet is a virtual world and it has nothing to do with the real world.

Q：How do you think of making friends online?

A：Well，I think it has two sides. It has a bright side and dark side. The bright side is that I can make lots of friends，learn lots of new things from them especially for English learners like me，we could practice English with those foreign friends. The dark side is it is still a virtual world. So we might make some bad friends without knowing it.

Q：What kinds of TV programme do you like watching?

A：Among all the TV programmes，I love quiz shows，talk shows and entertainment shows most. I guess it is because they can broaden my horizons / eyes，enrich my knowledge and the time I watch TV with my family is the most precious time.

其他类似题目：
- Do you read news? Newspaper or TV?
- What is your favorite topic in news?
- What is the most important thing in news?

6）关于兴趣

Q：What do you do in your free time?

A：A lot of things. For example，playing sports with friends，dating with my boyfriend or reading some good books.

A：Well，usually I like finding a fancy / nice tea house to do some reading and enjoy some high quality tea such as Longjing tea which is very famous in Hangzhou or even the whole country.

Q：Do you have any hobbies?

A：Yes，sure，people all have their hobbies. Some like reading，but I prefer dancing. I started to learn dance ten years ago when I was in primary school. No matter how busy I am，I'll try to manage to practice dancing at least two hours every day. I'm really keen on it.

A：Well，I'm not a person that has a lot of hobbies. In fact，collecting is the only thing I'd like to view as my hobby in my life. I bet you would not believe that I'm actually collecting various candy wraps. You may feel that candy wraps are children's thing not an adult like me. But，I'm just keen on those colourful wraps. Sometimes，I even can tell a story based on them. It's like I'm able to experience their vivid life.

A：Though I play many different types of sports，my best love is，however，basketball. I've been playing it regularly for three years since if came to high school and I am crazy about it.

Q：What do you do with your friends in your leisure time?

A：Err. Usually we'll find a fancy club to grab couple of drinks or go to play basketball. But，recently all of us are pretty busy with study. We haven't hung out for almost a month.

Q：Do you like fashion?

A：No，I'm not a fashion follower. I just choose what I like and honestly，I don't really understand fashion.

Q：Do you like sports?

A：I'm not a sporty type person as you can see from my appearance. But sometimes I do like jogging along the West Lake. Watching the willows dancing gently in the breeze，enjoying the lotus flowers blossoming in the water. That feels good.

Q：Do you like films?

A：Yes! I'm a big fan. I like watching all kinds of films from comedies to horror movies，from romance to adventure movies and action movies are my favourite.

A：Err，I'm not very into movies but sometimes I do like to watch several documentaries produced by BBC because I can learn various things about other cultures.

Q：Do you like to see films in a cinema or at home?

A：I prefer to see films at home. One of the reasons is I could control the film myself. I could fast forward or pause it whenever I want. It is a freedom that you can't enjoy if you go to cinema. And best of all，I can invite friends over to join me without having to pay for their tickets.

A：Well，it makes no difference to me. Watching films in a cinema is good for the fact that the sound effects are just excellent while enjoying a movie at home also has its advantages because I can be more relaxed and nobody would care that I eat crisps and make lots of noise.

Q：How often do you watch a film?

A：Well，I never count it. Maybe once a month because I'm so busy with my study / job that seldom have time for movies.

A：As I said before，I'm a huge fan of film. So I'll try to watch movies whenever I'm free. Sometimes one film each day and sometimes even more.

7）关于科技

Q：Do you have a mobile phone?

A：Yes，I do. In fact，I just got a new one yesterday. It's a smart phone and I can do a lot of things with it such as checking my emails and chatting with my friends all the time.

Q：Do you like flying?

A：Yes，I do like traveling by plane. It's fast and convenient. Also，I feel very excited about the food on plane such as orange juice and salty nuts.

A：No，not at all. I always feel uncomfortable when I am on the plane. Sometimes I even doubt that I may have claustrophobia.

Q：Which do you prefer? Traveling by train or by air?

A：Definitely the former one. As I said before，I don't like airplanes. Traveling by train makes me feel safer.

A：I'll go for plane because it shortens the time that I spend on the way to my destination. More importantly，I can see a lot of beautiful flight attendants.

还有一些考试中出现过比较奇怪的题目，也归纳如下：

Q：Do you like parks?

A：Yes, I like parks because they are great places to relax. I think all cities need green areas.

Q：Do you think different colours can change our moods?

A：Well, I do believe that colours can change our moods. For example, bright colours, like red, can make you feel energetic. Some greens and blues can be more relaxing.

Q：When do people give flowers in your country?

A：Well, it's not very popular for Chinese people to give flowers but we may do it occasionally, for example, boys will give flowers to their girlfriends on Valentine's Day. Also, people like visiting patients in hospital with flowers.

Q：Are your friends mostly your age or different ages?

A：Most of my friends are about the same age as me because we met at school or university. I've got one or two friends who are older or younger that I met through work.

Q：In what ways are your friends important to you?

A：I think it's important to have friends that you can talk to and share experiences with. My friends make me laugh, but I know I can also rely on them whenever I need help or support.

Q：What kinds of thing make you laugh?

A：I laugh most when I'm with friends talking about funny things that have happened to us. I also like watching comedians and comedy films.

Q：Do you think it's important for people to laugh?

A：Yes, of course. It's important to see the funny side of things; humour helps us not to take life too seriously. I think that laughter is good for our health.

Q：Is laughing the same as feeling happy?

A：It's not exactly the same because you can be happy without laughing, and sometimes we laugh when something bad has happened; a sense of humour can help us to cope with difficult situations.

第五章 雅思口语第二部分——问题卡片

雅思口语考试第二部分介绍

雅思口语考试第一部分结束以后,你会进入第二部分的考试环节。第二部分的考试时间大约为 3 到 5 分钟。考官将要求考生就某一话题做一段个人陈述,时间为 1 到 2 分钟。考官会给考生准备一张话题提示卡,上面有考生所需要表达的内容或者表明的观点,在拿到提示卡后考生有 1 分钟的时间进行准备。考生可以在这 1 分钟内记录一些笔记。

在反复通过对雅思口语考试的研究和分析之后,我们将口语考试中第二部分个人陈述类的话题分为四个种类:1) 人物类;2) 地点类;3) 物品类;4) 事件类。

根据以上四大类型,我们总结提炼出了针对话题的高分语言公式,通过传授答题结构,高分语言语法点来帮助考生解决如何说以及说什么的难点。

第二部分高分公式介绍

第一节 人物类话题

在本节中,我们将通过对人物类话题公式的讲解以及运用让同学们学会如何在雅思口语考试中描述一个人。

真题样题:

题一:Describe a famous person you admire

You should mention:

Who the person is and where he / she lives

What the person does

Why you admire this person and what you think people can learn from this person

题二:Describe someone you particularly enjoy working with

You should say:

What this person does

What kind of work you do with this person ·

How long you have worked with him / her and explain why you like working with this person

题三：Describe one of your school friends

You should say：

How you made friends with each other

Why you still remember him / her and what impression he / she has imposed on you

　　从样题中我们发现每个大题目下面都会有几个小题目,目的是为了给考生启发。我们应该注意的是,在以往的考试中我们发现提示题目中的内容不是必须成为考生陈述的重点内容,考生一样可以对提示外内容进行陈述。但是同时提示题目中的信息点需要考生在陈述中最好不要遗漏,否则会影响考试分数。

　　陈述结构公式：在解答人物类话题过程中,考生可以按照以下结构公式进行陈述：

Step 1: Say who is the person（and what this person is like）(optional)

步骤1：介绍你想描述的人是谁(以及这个人大概什么样子）(可选择)

Step 2: Say what this person does and how you know this person

步骤2：介绍这个人的职业以及你们是怎么认识的

Step 3: Say something happened between you and this person

步骤3：介绍一件发生在你和这个人之间的事情

Step 4: Say how this person influenced you or how you feel about this person

步骤4：介绍这个人是如何影响你或者你对这个人的感受是什么

　　答案范例解析：我们通过样题一作为例子来解析如何根据公式完成陈述

题一：Describe a famous person you admire

You should mention：

Who the person is and where he / she lives

What the person does

Why you admire this person and what you think people can learn from this person

Interviewer：Tell me about a famous person you admire

Step 1：Say who is the person

Student：Thomas Edison is one of the famous people I admire most. He is one of the most intelligent person in the world. Some people even said his brain is different from everyone else. He is a great scientist and inventor. He had made great contribution to the world.

Step 2：Say what this person does and how you know this person

Student：I first knew him when I was studying at primary school. In the class，our teacher told us he was thought to be a fool by his teacher when he was young. He was just full of imagination. He was also so diligent and determined that he worked day and night. These personalities made him attractive.

Step 3：Say something happened between you and this person

Student：After I learned his story I think his successes can be best explained by his famous saying "Genius is one percent inspiration and ninety-nine percent perspiration." which I have taken as my motto.

Step 4：Say how this person influenced you or how you feel about this person

Student：I admire him for his enviable contribution as well. It's unbelievable that he had made more than 1,000 inventions in his life. Edison has been an inspiration to me and has strengthened my belief in "As a man sows, so he shall reap".

介绍人物的高分细节：

> 1）正确地运用表示职业、身份、地位等用来描述人物的词汇。如：My grandfather once told me … / A professor in the university once said …
> 2）正确运用"who"引导的定语从句，补充人物描述信息。如：Alex, who was born in Hangzhou, often taught in Nanjing.
> 3）正确运用过去进行时和一般过去时描述你与人物之间的相识。如：When I was studying at the university, my brother introduced her to me.

下面我将针对以上高分细节来进行说明：

高分细节一：描述人物职业，社会地位，人物关系

首先我们来看几个例子：

Interviewer：Tell me about a famous person you admire

Student：Thomas Edison is one of the famous people I admire most. He is one of the most intelligent people in the world. Some people even said his brain is different from everyone else. He is a great scientist and inventor. He had made great contribution to the world.

Interviewer：Tell me about a person you particularly enjoy working with

Student：I have a part-time job as assistant in the Post-Graduate Office in my university. During this time, I have become acquainted with a post graduate who was also a part-time worker there.

Interviewer：Tell me about a friend of yours in your school

Student：My best friend is one of my high school classmates, who named Ding Ling. The way we became friends sounds like a legend.

从以上例子我们看出，在文中通过运用一些特定的词汇可以很好地反映你所描述及刻画的人物与你的关系，以及他／她本人的职业和社会地位。以下我们给大家补充一些常见基本的该类词汇：

Relatives：great-grandfather，grandparents，aunt，uncle，cousin，brother-in-law，mother-in-law，stepfather，nephew

Occupations：surgeon，accountant，architect，civil servant，plumber，electrician，butcher，self-employed，waiter / waitress，actor / actress，doctor，nurse，engineer

Relationship：celebrity，star，politician，TV presenter，sports personality，friend of the family，(ex-)boyfriend，distant relatives

练习：用下列给出词语完成句子

actress　friend of family　ex-girlfriend　TV presenter　self-employed　stepfather

1. Li Gong is probably the most popular _____ in China.
2. The first time I met my _____ is at my mother's wedding.
3. Alex has the _____ for years, my whole family like and trust him very much.
4. I don't like to watch the show " I love remembering lyrics" because I can't stand the _____ who hosts the programme.
5. I never speak to my _____ , she hurt me and left with another guy.
6. He doesn't need a job because he is _____ .

高分细节二：使用 who 引导的定语从句补充人物信息

Interviewer：Tell me about a person you particularly enjoy working with

Student：I have a part-time job as assistant in the Post-Graduate Office in my university. During this time, I have become acquainted with a post-graduate who was also a part-time worker there.

Interviewer：Tell me about a friend of yours in your school

Student：My best friend is one of my high school classmates, who named Ding Ling. The way we became friends sounds like a legend.

从以上两个例子我们看出，运用 who 引导的定语从句来向考官提供所描述人物的具体信息和细节是一种非常常用的高分语言点。在 who 引导的定语从句中我们有限定性和非限定两种从句形式：

第一种：who 引导的非限定性定语从句

My father, who worked as a civil servant for many years, thoroughly dislikes pop music.

Her good friend Alex, who became a very successful business man, had taught her English once.

在这两句例句中我们可以发现，非限制性定语从句所给出的额外的信息，在句子不占主导地位，将其从句子中省去语句依然通顺、成立。如："My father thoroughly dislikes pop music."在口语对话过程中，我们可以在插入的非限制性定语从句的起始和结尾处都稍作停顿,加强口语化。

第二种:who 引导的限定性定语从句

The girl who sits next to me is named Qin Lin.

The movie star who just won the Oscar will be in Hangzhou next week.

在这一组例句当中 who 引导的从句不再仅仅是给出额外的信息,相反的句子当中的信息起到确定人物的作用同时句子中不可省去从句部分,不然句子意思就不完整。如:"The girl is named Qin Lin."句子 "The girl" 到底指的是谁就不知道了。

练习:将打乱的词语组成句子

1. The are who football from one boys playing are class

   _____

2. Obama a on me who president of American impression was the made deep

   _____

3. The was strict math school at us taught who particularly teacher

   _____

4. My Shanghai told me sad news that friend who in lived

   _____

5. A caught lived home his policeman who near once stealing him fruit

   _____

高分细节三:使用过去进行时和一般过去时描述你与某人的相遇

在介绍某人的时候经常会介绍在什么时间、什么场合、什么情景之下相遇并认识了。在英语中能够将上述情景表达清楚的就是过去进行时和过去时。我们来看个例子:

Student:I first knew him when I was studying at primary school. In the class, our teacher told us he was thought to be a fool by his teacher when he was young. He was just full of imagination. He was also so diligent and determined that he worked day and night. These personalities made him attractive.

在例子中学生就是运用了过去进行时和一般过去时来进行表达。接下来我们来讲解两种时态的用法:

过去进行时:Be(过去时态)+ verb-ing

I was thinking …

They were talking about …

在过去进行时和过去时态中,when 和 while 经常充当桥梁作用。

When I was sleeping on my bed, my best friend called me and told me to go to the shop.

While my brother was playing game in his house, he noticed the earthquake.

练习：单项选择

1. My brother was visiting the city which his future girl friend lived in _____ they met.
   A. when   B. while   C. then

2. I gave my mum a call for help when she _____ cooking the dishes.
   A. were   B. was   C. is

3. We were _____ at university when we joined the same club and started socializing.
   A. study   B. studied   C. studying

4. My roommate was _____ her friend and so after a few weeks we were introduced to each other.
   A. dating   B. date   C. dated

5. My mother met my father while they were _____ around the country.
   A. travel   B. traveling   C. travelled

形容人物的高分细节：

> 1）正确运用词汇描述人的样貌和性格。如：My father is a very serious man. / Alex is quite humorous and open-minded.
>
> 2）正确运用过去进行时、过去完成时、一般过去时描述过去发生在人物身上的事情。如：He had studied abroad for many years thus after he returned, he looked so different.
>
> 3）正确运用频率副词来描述过去和现在的行为。如：I often like to go to our neighbor's home to listen to his story.

下面针对以上高分细节来进行说明：

高分细节一：正确运用词汇描述人物样貌和性格。在介绍某人的时候，对于人物的样貌以及性格的介绍往往是一种非常好的开始方式。

我们来看几个例子。

Student：... My grandpa is a very serious and kind man. His hair — as far back as I can remember — has always been a brilliant white but he is quite self-conscious about this ...

Student：... She was a large woman, about 5 feet and 8 inches and quite fat. When people saw her, they would be struck immediately by the expression on her face, which often appeared to be a scowl ...

以上两个例子都对人物进行了样貌以及性格的大致描述，让我们很快对人物的形象有了一个生动的了解。

补充一些样貌以及性格的词汇：

样貌类：

●nose：big / high / pointed / high-bridged / straight

● face：well-featured / handsome / bony / rosy / long / broad / beautiful

● eyes：sexy / sharp / slitty / watery / deep-sunken / big / bright

● mouth：fine / sensuous / small / big / mean

● ears：angular / thick / cauliflower / long-lobed / drooping

● hair：curly / straight / short / long / blonde

● figure：slender / small / plump / fat / muscularity / of medium weight / of medium height

性格类：

● funny：humorous / witty / funny / hilarious / amusing / hysterical

● shy：reserved / introverted / quiet / sensitive / conservation / timid

● confident：ambitious / self-assured / extroverted / adventurous / arrogant

● happy：charming / cheerful / vivacious / lively

● helpful：considerate / supportive / sympathetic

● honest：frank / reliable / sincere / straight-forward

● kind：gentle / calm / generous / loving / thoughtful

● intelligent：clever / bright / mature / talented / wise

练习:请大家运用以上的词汇对身边的同学以及老师进行样貌以及性格的描述,并将所用词汇进行记录。

高分细节二:频率副词用来描述人物的日常行为习惯以及爱好,在雅思口语考试中会被反复地运用到。我们来看几个例子:

Student：... when I think of my friend Lisa's appearance，the first thing which stands out is her constantly smiling face ...

Student：... Liang was originally from Shanxi and had a very strong Shanxi accent and was never without a cigarette ...

以上两个例子中都应用了频率副词对人进行描述,使人物更加立体。接下来看一些常用频率副词：

1) constantly / frequently / regularly / typically / commonly / often / sometimes / occasionally / rarely / seldom / hardly ever / almost never / always / usually / generally / every now and then / from time to time

2) times＋time period：once a day / twice a week / three times a month / four times a year

3) every＋time：every morning / every day at 9 p.m. / every birthday

练习：用已给词语造句

1) constantly

_____

2) occasionally

_____

3) every now and then

_____

4) seldom

_____

5) twice a month

_____

高分细节三：用过去进行时和一般过去时描述过去发生在人物身上的小故事

在描述的过程中，通过描述发生在人物身上有趣的小故事来例证人物性格特征，增加语言亮点，扩充文章长度是雅思口语考试中一种很讨巧很容易掌握并被广泛推荐使用的方法。那么，在描述过去事件的时候考生需要熟练掌握一般过去时和过去完成时以避免错误。

在前面的内容中我们已经讲解了一般过去时和过去进行时，现在我们来解析过去完成时：

过去完成时的结构为：had＋past participle

I had forgotten my pen at home.

They had decided that they would . . .

过去完成时的核心语法点为，过去完成时是用来描述发生在一般过去时之前的动作的，如 " Last Chinese new year, I had eaten a perfect meal in my grandma's house and then my mum made me eat her fruit salad. " 例句中"我是先在奶奶家吃饭，然后吃妈妈做的水果色拉"，两个动作都是发生在去年这个过去时间中，所以先发生的动作要用过去完成时。

练习:单项选择

1. He asked me _____ during the summer holidays.

   A. where I had been   B. where I had gone

   C. where had I been   D. where had I gone

2. What _____ Jane _____ by the time he was served?

   A. did, do   B. has, done   C. did, did   D. had, done

3. I _____ 900 English words by the time I was ten.

   A. learned   B. was learning   C. had learned   D. learnt

4. She _____ lived here for _____ years.

   A. had, a few   B. has, several

   C. had, a lot of   D. has, a great deal of

5. By the time my parents reached home yesterday, I _____ the dinner already.

   A. had cooked   B. cooked   C. have cooked   D. was cooked

6. She said she _____ the principle already.

   A. has seen   B. saw   C. will see   D. had seen

7. She said her family _____ themselves _____ the army during the war.

   A. has hidden, from   B. had hidden, from

   C. has hidden, with   D. had hidden, with

8. By the time he was ten years old, he _____.

   A. has completed university   B. has completed the university

   C. had completed an university   D. had completed university

9. She had written a number of books _____ the end of last year.

   A. for   B. in   C. by   D. at

10. He _____ to play _____ before he was 11 years old.

    A. had learned, piano   B. had learned, the piano

    C. has learned, the piano   D. learns, piano

阐述影响的高分细节:

> 1)正确运用与实际事实相反的条件句型来反映人物对你的重要性。如:If I hadn't met her I would never have . . .
>
> 2)正确运用现在完成时来谈论人物的变化和成就。如:She has taught me to be confident to face the world. / Alex has had a great influence on my life.
>
> 3)能在口语表达中运用一些国外的俚语、俗语、名人名言等地道的语言。如:Me and my best friend Lee usually yap about school, family, friends and life in general.

下面将针对以上高分细节来进行说明：

高分细节一：正确运用与实际事实相反的条件句型来反映人物重要性

Student：... My grandpa had been an army man for many years and I think if it hadn't been for him, I would never join the army ...

Student：... I am sure I wouldn't have studied a master's degree in movie directing if I hadn't watched his movie ...

例子中通过对于条件句型的运用，实际上强调了人物对于你的重要性，更让人觉得有信服力。接下来我们分析一下第三条件句。

第三条件句的结构：

1）if＋had(n't)＋过去分词＋would(n't) have＋过去分词

如：If it hadn't been him I would have died already.

2）would(n't) have＋过去分词＋if＋had(n't)＋过去分词

如：I wouldn't have studied movie if I hadn't watched that movie.

以上两种结构都可以，条件句型用来描述事情和事实相反，往往可以解释原因。

如：If my teacher hadn't been so relaxed，I'm sure I would have studied harder.

实际意义上这句话表明的是老师那时候太放松了，所以我没用功读书。

If Bill Gates hadn't been so ambitious，he wouldn't have been so successful.

实际意义是正因为比尔·盖茨很有抱负，他才能变得那么成功。

练习：单项选择

1. If I _____ where he lived, I _____ a note to him.
   A. knew，would
   B. had known，would have sent
   C. know，would send
   D. knew，would have sent

2. If they _____ earlier than expected, they _____ here now.
   A. had started，would be
   B. started，might be
   C. had started，would have been
   D. will start，might have been

3. I didn't know his telephone number. _____ it, I _____ then.
   A. Had I known，would ring him up
   B. Should I know，would have rung him up
   C. If I knew，would ring him up
   D. Had I known，would have rung him up

4. Mary is ill today. If she _____, she _____ absent from school.
   A. were not ill，wouldn't be
   B. had been ill，wouldn't have been
   C. had been ill，should have been
   D. hadn't been ill，could be

5. Were I to do it, I _____ it some other way.
   A. will do
   B. would do
   C. would have done
   D. were to do

6. I _____ him the answer _____ possible，but I was so busy then.

    A. could tell，if it had been   B. must have told，were it

    C. should have told，had it been   D. should have told，should it be

7. Without your help，we _____ so much.

    A. won't achieve   B. didn't achieve

    C. don't achieve   D. wouldn't have achieved

8. You didn't take his advice. _____ his advice，you _____ such a mistake.

    A. Had you taken，wouldn't have made

    B. If you had taken，would make

    C. Were you lo take，shouldn't have made

    D. Have you taken，won't have made

9. We wish we _____ what you did when we were at high school.

    A. did   B. could have done

    C. have done   D. should do

10. She wishes she _____ to the theatre last night.

    A. went   B. would go   C. had gone   D. were going

11. Tom is very short now. His mother wishes that he _____ be tall when he grows up.

    A. could   B. should   C. would   D. were able to

12. My sister advised me that I _____ accept the invitation.

    A. could   B. must   C. should   D. might

13. He asks that he _____ an opportunity to explain why he's refused to go there.

    A. is given   B. must give   C. should give   D. be given

14. Do you think of Wang Fang's suggestion that he _____ Mr. Li to the party?

    A. will invite   B. have invited   C. is invited   D. invite

15. I insisted that he _____ at once.

    A. be gone   B. go   C. would go   D. might go

16. Li Ming insisted that he _____ anything at all.

    A. hadn't stolen   B. shouldn't steal   C. doesn't steal   D. steal

17. It is quite natural that my coming late again _____ them very angry.

    A. had made   B. would make   C. makes   D. make

18. He acted as if he _____ everything in the world.

    A. knew   B. knows   C. has known   D. won't know

19. Read it aloud so that I _____ you clearly.

    A. may hear   B. will hear   C. hear   D. have heard

20. They got up early in order that they _____ they first train.

    A. caught   B. will catch   C. might catch   D. shall catch

高分细节二：用现在完成时描述变化和成就

Student：... My mother has always taught me to be more patient and understanding towards others.

Student：... Obama has become the first Africa-American president in the United States history.

现在完成时的结构：have＋过去分词

如：She has become one of the most famous actresses in the world.

Alex has had a great influence on my life.

练习：用现在完成时翻译下列中文句子

1）姚明已经成为了第一个在 NBA 打球的中国人。

_____

2）我的老师一直告诉我们要相信自己，尽自己最大的努力。

_____

3）我的父亲一直陪伴在我的身边，鼓励并支持着我。

_____

4）尽管我已经做了很多让老师失望和生气的事情，但是老师还是没有放弃我。

_____

5）李博士已经在这个领域中有了多年的经验，正因如此他今天才能这么成功。

_____

高分细节三：当表达对别人敬佩的时候考生往往需要描述这个人的成绩，在表达成就的同时能用一些地道的表达方式能给考官带来良好的印象。接下来我们补充一些地道的表示成就的短语：

1）working hard：through sheer hard work / to struggle for something / to fight for something / to have the determination to do something / to stand up for something / to show perseverance

例句：My father fought for everything he has achieved.

2）success：to have the will to success / to have a desire for success / to climb the ladder of success / to get a lucky break

例句：Slowly but surely，Alex climbed the ladder of success and finally reached the top position.

3）talented：to have a gift for doing something / to develop his / her talent for doing something

例句：Johnny has really developed his talent as a laugh-making star.

表达敬仰和感情的高分细节:

> 1）正确使用表示敬仰的词句。如:I love her because . . . / I will always admire him because . . .
>
> 2）正确使用榜样、偶像的表达方式。如:Mum will always be the hero in my heart.

下面将针对以上高分细节来进行说明:

高分细节一:如何表示敬仰和钦佩

Student：I admire him for his enviable contribution as well. It's unbelievable that he had made more than 1,000 inventions in his life. Edison has been an inspiration to me and has strengthened my belief in "As a man sows, so he shall reap".

Student：. . . although I didn't become a movie director myself, I feel that Feng Xiaogang had a very positive impact on my development. For me, he is the best teacher I ever had.

在描述人物的过程中,考生需要在考试中对人物为什么特别、为什么值得敬仰给出解释。我们来看一些表达方式:

- I love her because . . .
- I really appreciate what he has done for our nation.
- I look up to her due to the reason that . . .
- The teacher all thinks highly of him and his work.
- His parents must be very proud of his achievement that . . .

练习:请运用下列词汇造句来表达对人的敬仰和钦佩

1）greatly admire

_____

2）in high regard

_____

3）special to me

_____

4）looked up to

_____

5）felt proud

_____

6）appreciate

_____

高分细节二:榜样和偶像的表述方式

我们来看两个例子:

Student:... Edison has been an inspiration to me and has strengthened my belief in "As a man sows, so he shall reap ...

Student:... my grandpa was a great role model for me when I was growing up ...

我们来补充一些偶像、榜样的说法:

• Idol

例句:Michel Jackson, who is always a legend, was my hero when I was young.

• Hero

例句:My father was my hero for many years.

• Pop icon

例句:"Brother Sharp" became a big pop icon. He was all over the media.

• Charismatic Leader

例句:Nelson Mandela, who was imprisoned for fighting for human rights in South Africa, was a charismatic leader in his country.

• Inspiration

例句:Some say that the B. S. B. was not only a talented boy-band, but they were inspirations for their generation.

在人物类话题的最后我们再次来复习一下答题的结构:

Step 1:Say who is the person (and what this person is like)(optional)

步骤1:介绍你想描述的人是谁(以及这个人大概什么样子)(可选择)

Step 2:Say what this person does and how you know this person

步骤2:介绍这个人的职业以及你们是怎么认识的

Step 3:Say something happened between you and this person

步骤3:介绍一件发生在你和这个人之间的事情

Step 4:Say how this person influenced you or how you feel about this person

步骤4:介绍这个人如何影响你或者你对这个人的感受是什么

请考生在按照结构回答的同时将我们在书中所解析以及练习的高分语言细节运用在考题之内,这样能帮助考生尽可能地达到想要的分数。下列考试真题请认真练习:

1. Describe a famous musician you admire

   You should explain: who this person is

   What is he / she famous for

   What he / she composed and what you think about him / her

2. Describe a character in a film or a TV show

   You should say: How old he / she is

   Which film or show he / she is from

What his / her personality is and explain why you like / dislike this character

3. Describe a person you want to be like

   You should say: Who he / she is

   What kind of person he / she is and why you want to be like him / her

4. Describe a talkative person you know

   You should say: Who the person is

   How talkative he / she is and whether you like him / her

5. Describe a person you met who speaks another language

   You should say: Who the person is

   When and where you met this person

   What this person is like and explain how you communicate with him / her

6. Describe your own personality

   You should say: What your personality is

   What the strong points of your personality are

   and why you think you have such a personality

7. Describe a teacher who has influenced you in your education

   You should say: What subject he / she taught

   What the teacher looks like

   What the teacher's personality is

   What special about him / her and explain why the teacher has influenced you

8. Describe a family (not your family) that you know well

   You should say: Where this family lives

   Who the members of the family are

   How you knew them and explain how you feel about this family

第二节　地点类话题

在本节中,我们将通过对地点类话题公式的讲解以及运用让同学们学会如何在雅思口语考试中描述一个地点。

首先我们来看一些地点类的真题:(提示小题省略)

- Describe a memorable city you have visited
- Describe a place with a lot of water
- Describe a museum，library or exhibit in your hometown
- Describe an important historical place in your country

陈述结构公式:在解答地点类话题过程中,考生可以按照以下结构公式进行陈述:

Step 1：Say what it is and where it is
步骤1:介绍这个地点是什么以及它所处的位置
Step 2：Say what this place looks like
步骤2:介绍这个地方看上去是什么样子的
Step 3：Say what this place is for
步骤3:介绍这个地点是用来做什么的
Step 4：Say why this place is special and how you feel about it
步骤4:介绍这个地点有什么特殊的或者你对这个地点的感受是什么

答案范例解析:我们通过样题一作为例子来解析如何根据公式完成陈述
题一:Describe the most interesting building in your country
You should say：where it is located
What it is used for and why you think it is the most interesting one

Interviewer：Tell me about the most interesting building in your country

Step 1：Say what it is and where it is
Student：I think the most interesting building in China is the Temple of Heaven. It is located in southern Beijing and it was built in 1420，the 18th year of the reign of Ming Emperor Yongle.

Step 2：Say what this place looks like
Student：The temple of heaven has two parts — the inner altar and outer altar. The main buildings are the Circular Mound Altar at the southern end. The Circular Mound Altar is a three-tier white stone terrace enclosed by ways. The altar has taiji rock at the center of the top terrace.

Step 3：Say what this place is for
Student：The temple was the place where emperors went to worship heaven for good

harvests. In 1998，UNESCO had the Temple of Heaven solemnly listed as one of the world's legacies.

Step 4：Say why this place is special and how you feel about it

Student：The most interesting thing is that if you stand on the rock and speak in your normal voice，your voice will sound louder and more resonant to yourself than to others around you. That is because the sound waves reflected by the balustrades are bounced back to the center by the round wall.

介绍地点高分细节：

> 1）正确介绍地点的名称。如：The Bird's Nest，The Summer Palace
>
> 2）正确的介绍地点的位置。如：It is close to the Chinese restaurant ... / It is located in the center of the town.

高分细节一：正确介绍地点名称

我们来补充一些特殊地点名称的词汇：

◉Tourism：tourist attraction / historic site / palace / museum

◉Shopping：shopping mall / shopping center / plaza / market / discount store

◉Accommodation：house / flat / apartment / campsite / mansion

◉Entertainment：bar / nightclub / theatre / cinema / concert hall / music hall

◉Leisure：gym / sports ground / stadium / pitch /

◉Natural：park / garden / nature reserve / countryside

◉Religious：mosque / temple / church / cathedral

练习　请你列举你周围的下列地点

1）Temple：

_____

2）Shopping Mall：

_____

3）Historical Site：

_____

4）Mansion：

_____

5）Nightclub：

高分细节二：正确描述地点的位置

首先我们来看几个例子：

Student：... Jingzhou is located on the middle reaches of the Yangtze River ...

Student：... The Regent Hotel is oriented to the Southwest，with its windows looking out directly upon the intersection of Mishi Avenue and Jinbao Street ...

从以上例子中我们发现，在描述地点的文章中，考生一般都会被要求描述地点的位置。以下我们来分析一下可以如何描述地点的位置：

◉A 在 B 的东方/西方/南方/北方

A is / lies / is located / is situated in / on / to the east / west / south / north of B

（in 表示 A 在 B 内部，on 表示 A 和 B 接壤，to 表示 A 和 B 分开）

◉A 在 B 内部的某个部位

A is in the eastern / southern / western / northern part of B.

◉A 在 B 西北部的 120 千米处

A lies 120 km to the northwest of B.

◉A 在 B 的……角落

A is at / in the south-eastern corner of B.（at 表示 A 在 B 外部，in 表示 A 在 B 内部）

◉在河流或道路的南边/北边等

on the south / southern side of the river

on both sides of the road

on the other side

◉临近马路的地区

the area adjacent to / near / next to / just off the road

◉在道路或河流的最南端

at the southern end of the river

◉A 在 B 的对面

A is on the opposite side of B.

A is opposite B.

◉A 在 B 东部的边界上（A 在 B 外部）

A is on the eastern border of B.

◉A 在 B 东部边缘上（A 在 B 内部）

A is on / along the eastern edge of B.

练习　选词填空

> in, on, beside, under, above, next to, in front of, behind, between

1. Beijing is _____ the north of China.
2. The twins usually stand _____ their parents，and their parents are in the middle.
3. There is a map of China _____ the wall of our classroom.
4. Before 2000，there was no airline _____ the two cities.

5. The boy sitting _____ Tina，so she couldn't see the film clearly.

6. She will leave her homework _____ the teacher's desk after school today.

7. You must ride your bike _____ the right side of the road.

8. Mr Smith lives _____ that building. His house is _____ the fifth floor.

9. There was an exciting moment in our class when a large bird flew _____ the room.

10. The boy is taller than his friend，so he sits _____ him in the classroom.

11. The flowers are _____ the vase on the desk.

12. She is the tallest one. She always sits _____ the back row.

13. He put a painting on the wall _____ the sofa.

14. The teacher's desk is _____ the front of the classroom.

描述地点样子的高分细节：

> 1）正确应用描述尺寸、形状的词汇。如：The Bird's Nest is giant and tall. / The Yellowstone Park is a vast open space in USA.
>
> 2）正确描述地点特征和外观。如：The Temple of Heaven has two parts —— the inner altar and outer altar.
>
> 3）正确运用连词。如：In addition to having hosted the Olympic swimming contests，the Water Cube is also a fascinating piece of architecture.

在样题一中我们已经发现了考生对天坛的结构以及外观做了非常详细的描述，这是在介绍地点的时候非常容易扩充文章长度的方式，所以鼓励考生们掌握。接下来补充一些关于形状和尺寸的词汇：

尺寸类：

● Big：huge / large / massive / vast / enormous / immense

● Small：tiny / minuscule / cramped / squat / little

● Width：wide / broad / thin / thick

● Height：high / tall / short / low / squat

● Length：short / long / winding / endless / far-reaching

形状类：

● 十字形：cross / with a cross

● 三角形：triangle / triangular

● 四边形：quadrangle / quadrangular

● 矩形：rectangle / rectangular

● 长方形：oblong / oblong

● 正方形：square / square

● 菱形：diamond / rhomboidal

● 梯形：trapezoid / trapezium —— trapezoid / trapezoidal

●多边形：polygon / polygonal

练习　搭配完成词组

1) A _____ mountain range　　　　winding
2) A _____ building　　　　　　　vast
3) A _____ shopping complex　　　massive
4) A _____ path　　　　　　　　　tiny small
5) A _____ window　　　　　　　　tall

高分细节二：表达特征和外观的方式

首先让我们来看两个考生实例：

Student：... as for me, the West Lake is a beautiful and amazing place which represents the best culture of Hangzhou and history. The lake was surrounded by a number of hills on which are various examples of traditional Chinese architecture ...

Student：... indeed, Zhiweiguan Restaurant provides an ideal place for students to get away from the cafeteria. Clean and tidy, with stylishly minimal interior decoration and soft lighting, it represents everything the cafeteria is not ...

从以上两个例子可以看出，考生在描述地点的过程中加入了对地点的特点和外观的介绍，使得描述更加形象具体。

以下我们来补充一些地道的形容地点外观的表述方式：

●Light：airy / bright / well-lit / clear

●Dark：dingy / gloomy / dim / murky

●Ugly：horrible / disgusting / awful / unappealing

●Beautiful：appealing / attractive / comfortable / comely

●Impressive：awe-inspiring / majestic / thrilling / significant / fabulous

●Untidy：crumbling / tatty / dusty / shabby / messy

●Age：old / ancient / new / modern / shining / antiquated

●Luxury：expensive / unmarked / posh / luxurious / opulent

练习　将下列句子翻译成英文

1) 夜晚，西湖上的小舟都被覆盖在明亮的夜灯下。

_____

2) 中央电视台新大楼已经因为它现代的造型成为了旅游者参观的景致。

_____

3) 我朋友的房间给人一种非常温暖的感觉，因为房间被漆成了橙黄色的。

_____

4) 因为房子那扇巨大的窗子的原因，所以房间里非常的明亮，一点都不觉得暗。

_____

5）南京是一个非常吸引人的城市,因为它有悠久的历史和优美的风景。

___

高分细节三: 表示并列、递进的关联词

我们先来看一个例子:

Student：... Suzhou is not only a beautiful city. You can not only enjoy the exquisite historic site, but also taste the modern lifestyle there ...

在列举地点的特征时应尽量避免用呆板的一,二,三来描述地点,而更应该尝试运用连接词将描述的意义段落进行更好地连接,使口语描述听起来更加的连贯流畅。

接下来我们来看一些常用的表示递进和并列的词组:

• as well as ... also ... / as well as verb-ing ... also ...

例句:As well as being a place of great natural beauty, it is also a place of great historical significance.

• besides ... also ...

例句:Besides being a place of great natural beauty, it is also a place of great historical significance.

• in addition to ... also ...

例句:In addition to being one of the most popular music venues in the city, the bar also has great food.

• along with ... also

例句:Along with great shops, Hangzhou Plaza also has some handy restaurants.

• both ... and ...

例句:This hotel is both conveniently located and reasonably priced.

练习:请用以下每组连词词组造一个与地点特征有关的句子

A. as well as ... also ... / as well as verb-ing ... also ...

___

B. besides ... also ...

___

C. in addition to ... also ...

___

D. along with ... also

___

E. both ... and ...

___

描述地点功用的高分细节：

> 1）正确运用被动语态表示功能和目的。如：The temple was the place where emperors went to worship heaven for good harvests.
>
> 2）描述过去的习惯来交代地点在你生活中的地位。如：If I felt depressed I would go to the gym and find a way to release my energy. ／ I used to sit in the part and enjoy the sunshine in the afternoon.
>
> 3）描述当地的特色与特产。如：He who has never been to the Great Wall is not a true man. ／ My hometown is famous for its Longjing Tea.

下面将针对以上高分细节来进行说明。

高分细节一：用被动语态描述某地的功用

我们先来看几个例子：

Student：... The temple was the place where emperors went to worship heaven for good harvests. In 1998，UNESCO had the Temple of Heaven solemnly listed as one of the world's legacies ...

Student：... it's used to collect，store，display，research，and exhibit historical and cultural relics from all over China，which was so influential to the history and culture of the Zhejiang region ...

以上两个例子中都用被动语态对地点的功用做了详细的描述，使考官对地点的认识更为理性化。在描述过程中通过对被动语态的运用使文章语态听起来更为多变复杂以达到追分的目的。下面我们来解析被动语态：

被动语态的结构：be（随时态变化而变化）＋过去分词

例句：The Pyramids of Egypt were constructed by slaves.

This museum was used to be a store once in the Second World War.

练习：

1. The People's Republic of China _____ on October 1，1949.

    A. found   B. was founded   C. is founded   D. was found

2. English _____ in Canada.

    A. speaks   B. are spoken   C. is speaking   D. is spoken

3. This English song _____ by the girls after class.

    A. often sings   B. often sang   C. is often sang   D. is often sung

4. This kind of car _____ in Japan.

    A. makes   B. made   C. is making   D. is made

5. New computers _____ all over the world.

    A. is used   B. are using   C. are used   D. have used

6. Our room must _____ clean.

   A. keep   B. be kept   C. to be kept   D. to keep

7. — I'd like to buy that coat.

   — I'm sorry, _____.

   A. it sold   B. it's selling   C. it's been sold   D. it had been sold

8. A new house _____ at the corner of the road.

   A. is building   B. is being built   C. been built   D. be building

9. The key _____ on the table when I leave.

   A. was left   B. will be left   C. is left   D. has been left

10. Doctors _____ in every part of the world.

   A. need   B. are needing   C. are needed   D. will need

高分细节二：描述过去的习惯

我们先来看两个例子：

Student：… near the window，there was a writing desk and a chair. I used to study there when I was a child …

Student：When I was a student in the Zhejiang University I always would like to go to the gym to release myself after a long day of studying …

以上的两个例子中考生通过对自己过去习惯的描述来侧面描写地点，拉近了地点与描述人之间的关系，侧面烘托了地点的特殊性。接下来我们来解析如何描述过去的习惯：

1）频率副词＋一般过去时

例句：I always go to that bar in order to meet some foreigners.

My grandparents go to that park regularly to do exercises.

2）used to

例句：I used to spend the whole afternoon enjoying the beautiful sunshine there.

My girl friend used to go to shop for my clothes.

3）条件状语从句

例句：If the class is noisy I would go to that garden to read.

If I need to practice my English I would go to that Starbucks to find foreigners.

练习　将下列中文翻译成英文

1）每年的暑假，我们全家都会去舟山海边游玩。

_____

2）如果我没课的话，我会经常在那个安静的咖啡馆里看书上网。

_____

3）爸爸过去常带着枪去那片林子打猎。

_____

4) 这里经常有一些小偷出现,我曾经在这里被偷过。

5) 我过去常常在这个公园的门口等我的女朋友。

高分细节三:描述当地的特色与特产

我们先来看两个例子:

Student:... My hometown is famous for its beautiful scenery such as West Lake. Thousands of people from all over the world come to visit it...

Student:... Shanghai is more of a place to go for business opportunities than a place to go for a visiting...

通过以上两个例子我们可以发现,考生可以在描述地点的过程中实际列举该地的特色或者特产来表达该地的特殊性。接下来我们来总结一下列举特色或特产的句型:

• be famous for＋$n.$ ／verb-ing

例句: This bar is famous for its drink.

• be renowned for＋$n.$ ／verb-ing

例句: Sichuan is renowned for cooking delicious spicy food.

• be note for＋$n.$ ／verb-ing

例句: The Great Wall is note for its size and historical importance.

• be popular with＋people

例句: This night club is only popular with some teenagers.

• be excellent for＋$n.$ ／verb-ing

例句: This university is excellent for its teaching facilities.

表达对某地感受的高分细节:

1) 正确运用表达感受的表达方式。如: It is important to me because... ／ I always like to... there.

2) 正确使用描述地点的形容词。如: The West Lake is a relaxing yet energizing place of natural beauty.

下面将针对以上高分细节来进行说明。

首先来看两个例子:

Student:... The library is important to me because we can borrow books, enjoy reading, and also surf the Internet in the library. It provides a lot of conveniences to us...

Student:... My grandparents are no longer with us now, but whenever I think of that house, I think of them, and it is a memory I treasure...

以上两个例子中,考生都描述了某地的感觉和情感,强调了地点的特殊性。那么我们来看一下在雅思口语考试中有哪些常用来描述感觉的句型：

- I like / love / value the place because ...

例句：I love the place because it's where I belong.

- The place is important to me because ...

例句：The place is important to me because it can remind me home.

- The place gives me with an impression of being ...

例句：The place gives me with an impression of being a student again.

- The place makes / lets me feel ...

例句：The British Museum always makes me feel inspired.

- The place provides me with ...

例句：The Legion Field provides me and my friends with a pleasant，green space in which to play sports or just hang out.

练习　运用以上句型对下列地点发表感想

1. 学校：

2. 祖国：

3. 酒吧：

4. 巴厘岛：

5. 卧室：

高分细节二：描述一个地方的形容词

我们先来看两个例子：

Student：... The Summer Palace is really important to me because it is so tranquil ...

Student：... In my point of view，the modern buildings in our country look very magnificent ...

以上两个例子中考生在形容地点的同时加上了许多修饰性的形容词来使语言更生动，描述更具体。接下来我们就来补充一些修饰地点的形容词：

- Relaxing：cosy / comfortable / quiet / peaceful / tranquil
- Interesting：enchanting / educational / inspiring / fascinating / engrossing
- Exciting：energizing / breathtaking / exhilarating / thrilling
- Beautiful：delightful / charming / magnificent / pretty / attractive
- Busy：hectic / chaotic / bustling / frantic / stressful

练习　选词填空

bustling，enchanting，cosy，comfortable，stressful

1）I usually love the _____ atmosphere of the market，though sometimes I can be a bit too hectic.

2）Friday woods is an _____ little forest where you can get a taste of nature.

3）I love Helen's Coffee Shop because it provides me with a _____ and _____ place to study.

在地点类话题的最后我们再次来复习一下答题的结构：

Step 1：Say what it is and where it is

步骤1：介绍这个地点是什么以及它所处的位置

Step 2：Say what this place looks like

步骤2：介绍这个地方看上去是什么样子的

Step 3：Say what this place is for

步骤3：介绍这个地点是用来做什么的

Step 4：Say why this place is special and how you feel about it

步骤4：介绍这个地点有什么特殊的或者你对这个地点的感受是什么

　　请考生在按照结构回答的同时将我们在书中所解析以及练习的高分语言细节运用在考题之内，这样能帮助考生尽可能地达到想要的分数。下列考试真题请认真练习：

• Describe the room you lived in when you were a child

You should explain：Where it was

What it looks like and how the room is arranged

• Describe a modern building in your country

You should say：What it is

What it looks like and what it is used for

• Describe a library in your university

You should say：What type of library it is

What books you often borrow there and what advantages and functions it has

• Describe a factory / company you have been to

You should say：Where it is

What it does and what facilities it has

• Describe an area of special natural beauty you have ever seen

You should say：Where it is

When you saw it and why it is special

第三节　物品类话题

　　在本节中,我们将通过对物品类话题描述结构的分析来掌握如何在雅思口语中正确有效地描述物品类话题。首先我们来看一些真题:

- Talk about something once you sold to someone
- Talk about something you made by your own hand
- Describe an invention you know and like
- Describe a gift you once receive in your childhood
- Describe a story you heard from someone

物品类话题描述结构:

Step 1: Say what it is and where did you get it (who did you get it from)

第一步:描述它是什么,你从哪里或者从谁那里得到它的

Step 2: Say what it looks like and what is its function

第二步:描述它的外观和功能是什么

Step 3: Say how it is

第三步:评价它到底怎么样

Step 4: Say why it is special and how you feel about it

第四步:描述为什么它很特殊以及你对它的感受

答案范例分析:

Describe your favorite gift

You should say: What it was

When you received it and why you like it the most

Interviewer: Talk about a favorite gift you received in your life

Step 1: Say what it is and where did you get it (who did you get it from)

Student: The first day I went to university, my mother bought me an electronic dictionary as gift. That is the best present I have ever received.

Step 2: Say what it looks like and what is its function

Student: It is silvery and so small that I could carry it in my pocket. My major is English, so my mother hoped that the electronic dictionary could help me to improve my English.

Step 3: Say how it is

Student: With this gift's help, I found I never have to worry about reading anymore. Every time when I found some words I don't understand then I can look into it at any time and any where I want. It is vey convenient and useful.

Step 4：Say why it is special and how you feel about it

Actually，it is the thought from my mum behind the present that counts. On that day，I promised I would never let my mother down. And with the encouragement and help of the electronic dictionary，I made such rapid progress that before long I got the scholarship of the semester. Therefore，I think it is the best gift I have ever received.

介绍物品背景及来历的高分细节：

> 1）正确运用间接宾语描述物品来历。如：My girlfriend bought me this suit. / I made her a doll.
>
> 2）正确运用一般过去时和过去进行时描述你怎么得到该物品的。如：When I was studying in the university my parents bought me a car.
>
> 3）正确使用描述物品外观的形容词。

下面我们将针对以上高分细节进行解析：

高分细节一：正确使用间接宾语描述物品来历

首先让我们来看两个实例：

Student：... my parents bought me my first laptop on my 18th birthday ...

Student：... I would like to talk about a gift I was given by my best friend Alex ...

通过以上两个实例我们发现在介绍物品的时候，作为基本信息描述物品的来历是一种常见方法。而通过正确使用间接宾语能很好并很有效地帮助我们。

间接宾语使用结构：

• Subject＋verb＋indirect object＋direct object

例句：He gave me that book.

I send her my letter.

• Subject＋verb＋direct object＋to / for＋indirect object

例句：He gave a book to me.

I bought a car for her.

备注：间接宾语指代的是句子中的接受者，直接宾语指代句子中的授予者。

练习：改正句子中的错误

1. I made she a toy.

2. I bought a mobile phone to my brother.

3. My friend wrote to I a letter.

4. It I gave to a classmate.

5. Them ask I to buy it to he.

高分细节二:正确使用一般过去时和过去进行时描述你如何得到某物的

我们先来看两个实例:

Student: ... my grandma bought me my first skirt when I was 6 years old ...

Student: ... while I was waiting for the New Year's celebration, my mother gave a mobile phone as her gift ...

从以上两个实例中可以知道,当描述物品的时候通常会用一般过去时和过去进行时来描述如何得到该物品的。

一般过去时和过去进行时的描述结构:

一般过去时+when / while+be(过去时)+verb-ing

例句: I got this gift when I was studying in the university.

My parents sent me this letter while they were living in another city.

While / when+be(过去时)+verb-ing+一般过去时

例句: While I was visiting my friends for Christmas, I got a great gift.

When I was traveling in France, I bought a lot of cloth.

备注:一般进行时后面可以用的动词必须是延续性动词,指动作可以持续发生一段时间的,如等待、烧饭、做作业等。

练习 将以下中文翻译成英文

1. 在上高中的时候我买了我的第一台电脑。

2. 爱迪生在 1879 年发明了第一个电灯泡。

3. 当我正在享受和男朋友一起的晚餐的时候,他拿出了给我买的钻石戒指。

4. 在我的生日当天我的朋友给我买了一本关于教育的书籍送给我。

5. 我正在专心读书的时候,他把为我准备的礼物递给了我。

高分细节三:正确使用描述物品外观的形容词

首先我们来看两个实例:

Student: ... It was a fairly simple kite: about a meter long, diamond shaped and it had four colors — red, blue, yellow and green. I think ...

Student: ... laptops nowadays are very light, compact and sleek laptops made of plastic which can be carried everywhere ...

从以上两个例子可以看出在描述物品的过程中我们一般会对物体的外观做一些简单的描述。这可以使被介绍的物品的形象通过语言传达得更具体和形象。

首先列举一些用来形容物品的形容词：

- Size：huge / enormous / tiny / little / miniature / compact / average-sized
- Colors：grey / gold / silver / gold / multi-colored / black and white / rainbow-colored
- Material：cardboard / cotton / golden / leather / silk / wooden / plastic
- Shape：round / square / rectangular / diamond-shaped / oval / curved / triangular / cylindrical
- Age：ancient / antique / aged / worn / brand-new / modern / new
- Origin：Chinese / American / Western / mass-produced / hand-made / factory-produced
- Opinion：handy / useful / useless / silly / terrible / ugly / cute / attractive

备注：当我们在同时运用这些形容词描述物品外观的时候，请注意句子的排列顺序。正确的排列顺序为：

看法＋尺寸＋年代＋形状＋颜色＋出处＋材料

例句：It is a beautiful，huge marble statue.

That is a strange old round green building.

练习 将下列单词按正确顺序排列

1. lighter antique handy a silver is it

2. dress silk red an elegant

3. book a interesting grey mass-produced

4. an ancient watch golden

5. a glass building modern spherical

描述物品功能的高分细节：

1）正确使用被动语态描述物品的制造和功能。如：Mobile phones are not only used for talking to people and sending text messages but also for surfing the Web，keeping a diary and even as alarm clocks.

2）正确运用描述用途的方法。如：Computer provides people with more approaches to communicate with others.

下面我们针对以上两个高分细节进行解析。

高分细节一:正确使用被动语态描述物品的制造和功能

首先我们来看两个实例:

Student:... air conditioner is used for keeping the temperature as you want it to be in the room and it makes our life quality much better than before ...

Student:... this book is not only valued for its content but also for the wishes contained in it ...

从以上两个例子可以发现,除了用正常语境介绍物品的功能之外,我们还经常在雅思口语考试中运用被动语态进行介绍。这样可以提高语句和结构的变化性。

在前面的内容中我们已经学过了被动语态的基本结构,接下来我们来看一下用被动语态描述被制造和功用的结构。

描述制造的结构:

be(随时态变化而变化)+过去完成时+(by+制造者)

例句:The airplane was invented by the Wright brothers.

The photo was taken before I was born.

描述功能的结构:

be(随时态变化而变化)+过去完成时+to do something

例句:The airplane was invented to help human to realize the dream of flying.

All the invention was created to make our life better.

练习:将下列句子改成被动语态

1. Leonardo da Vinci painted the *Mona Lisa*.

2. We not only use the MP3 player to listen to the music but also use it to store some data.

3. My father used this pen all his life,so it must be very important to him.

4. Human beings created cars in order to make the trip easier.

5. The Chinese first found that the gun powder can be used in battle.

高分细节二:正确描述用途的方式

首先我们来看两个实例:

Student:... air conditioner is used for keeping the temperature as you want it to be in the room and it makes our life quality much better than before ...

Student:... this book is not only valued for its content but also for the wishes contained in it ...

从上述两个例子可以知道，在雅思口语中当描述物品的用途时，我们会用一些特定的词组来进行描述，使描述听上去更加地道。

以下列举一些常见的描述用途的词组：

• is used to do / for verb-ing ...

例句：Microsoft is used for dealing with all kinds of difficult tasks.

• is useful for verb-ing

例句：The electronic dictionary is useful for developing my English.

• provides（people）with

例句：Computer provides people with more approaches to communicate with others.

• is appreciated because ...

例句：This facility is appreciated because of its convenience.

• is valued for ...

例句：This photo is valued for the memory in it.

练习：根据已给词汇造句

1. Internet　is appreciate with

2. jazz music　is valued for

3. watch　is　useful for

4. book　provides with

评价物品的高分细节：

> 1）正确运用评价物品的形容词。如：Air conditioners are so convenient because they are cheap and easy to control.
> 2）在评价物品时正确运用连词。如：Although computer has its own disadvantages，it still improved our life quality because ...
> 3）正确运用比较与对比的方式评价物品。如：A digital camera is certainly much more convenient than a traditional camera because ...

以下我们将针对上述高分细节进行解析。

高分细节一：正确运用评价物品的形容词

首先我们来看两个例子：

Student：... Although it wasn't such a valuable gift，I didn't mind because I was just pleased to receive such a memorable gift.

Student：... my mother's ring is an antique, high quality and charming which is an item of jewelry ...

从以上例子可以知道，当在评价物品的时候都需要添加一些用来修饰的形容词。在考试中很多同学在评价时反复地多次用同一个形容词，使得语言单一。接下来补充一些评价物品的形容词：

- Age：innovative / fashionable / advanced / outdated / old fashioned / dated /
- Appearance：vivid / colorful / attractive / charming / eye-catching / unappealing
- Value：over-priced / expensive / costly / reasonable / economical / cheap
- Quality：high quality / reliable / well made / poor /
- Use：useful / practical / convenient / informative / educative / helpful
- Importance：essential / vital / crucial / needless / unnecessary / superfluous / beneficial
- Size / Weight：heavy / bulky / light / thick / thin / soft / hard

练习　用给出词汇造句

1. advanced

2. eye-catching

3. economical

4. well made

5. informative

6. superfluous

7. bulky

高分细节二：在描述物品时正确运用连词

首先我们来看两个例子：

Student：... my family's photographs of me as a child are really embarrassing. Not only do I have weird hairstyle in many of them, but also I'm often naked ...

Student：... Despite their high cost, the last pair of shoes I bought does not have good quality；they broke within the first two months ...

从以上两个例子可以发现，连词的运用能更好地加强考生在描述物品过程中的结构逻辑性和语句连贯性。其实在雅思口语的任何一个话题考试中，连词的运用都是考生追求高分的有效途径。下面介绍一下英语中的常见连词类型：

1. 增补(Addition)

in addition, furthermore, again, also, besides, moreover, what's more, similarly, next, finally

2. 比较(Comparison)

in the same way, likewise, similarly, equally, in comparison, just as

3. 对照(Contrast)

whereas, in contrast, on the other hand, instead, however, nevertheless, unlike, even though, on the contrary, while

4. 因果(Cause and effect)

because, because of, for, since, due to, owing to, thanks to, as a result (of), accordingly, hence, so, thus

5. 强调(Emphasis)

certainly, above all, indeed, of course, surely, actually, as a matter of fact, chiefly, especially, primarily, in particular, undoubtedly, absolutely, most important

6. 让步(Concession)

although, though, after all, in spite of, nevertheless, still, provided, while it is true ...

7. 例证(Exemplification)

for example, for instance, that is, namely, such as, in other words, in this case, by way of illustration

8. 总结(Conclusion)

to sum up, to conclude, in a word, in short, in brief, all in all, in all, to put it in a nutshell, in summary

9. 推断(Inference)

therefore, as a result (of), consequently, accordingly, so, otherwise

备注:考生不仅要记住和运用这些单词,同时更重要的是搞清楚每个连词所表示的逻辑关系,以免在考试中因为连词错误导致表述被考官误解,因此在相关度上失分。

练习 单项选择

1. — I don't like reading _____ watching TV. What about you?

— I don't like reading all day, _____ I like watching TV plays.

   A. and, but   B. and, and   C. or, and   D. or, but

2. You won't know the value of the health _____ you lose it.

   A. until   B. after   C. when   D. because

3. We bought Granny a present, _____ she didn't like it.

   A. but   B. and   C. or   D. so

4. Study hard, _____ you will pass the exam.

   A. so   B. for   C. but   D. and

5. Put on more clothes, _____ you'll catch cold.

   A. and   B. for   C. or   D. but

6. My shoes are worn out, _____ I need new ones.

   A. so   B. if   C. because   D. and

7. He ran _____ fast _____ he won the race.

   A. enough, to   B. so, that   C. too, to   D. both, and

8. He is only ten months. He can _____ read _____ write.

   A. either, or   B. neither, nor   C. both, and   D. so, that

9. She said she might come _____ Saturday _____ Sunday.

   A. neither, nor   B. neither, or   C. too, to   D. so, that

10. If Tom _____ Mike asks for their car, tell him to come tomorrow.

   A. or   B. and   C. with   D. but

11. It was already ten o'clock _____ we got to the museum this morning.

   A. that   B. when   C. if   D. for

12. It's a long time _____ we met last.

   A. so   B. after   C. since   D. before

13. That math problem is _____ difficult _____ nobody can do it.

   A. too, to   B. very, that   C. so, that   D. very, but

14. I'll give her the message _____ she comes back.

   A. since   B. before   C. until   D. as soon as

15. _____ the teacher came into the classroom, many students were talking to each other.

   A. While   B. If   C. Since   D. When

16. People often mistake us for each other _____ we are twins.

   A. if   B. when   C. because   D. after

17. Could you tell me _____ in your home town in winter?

   A. if it often snowed   B. whether does it often snow

   C. if it often snow   D. whether it often snows

18. Are you sure _____ Mr. Li will come to your birthday party?

   A. if   B. that   C. for   D. when

19. _____ Lily _____ Lucy like singing.

   A. Either, or   B. Neither, nor

   C. Both, and   D. So, that

20. Read the sentences slowly _____ we can understand what you read.

   A. so that   B. before   C. until   D. because

高分细节三：正确运用比较与对比的方式评价物品

以下我们来看个例子：

Student：... Despite being slightly more expensive than a landline, mobile phones are so useful and convenient that many people simply couldn't do without one ...

从以上例子可以知道，在雅思口语考试中为了能更好地突出物品的优越性经常会在不同物品之间进行比较。而比较级是我们在其中必然会用到的一个语言点。接下来我们将对比较级的运用进行解析：

• 比较级的构成：

1．单音节形容词的比较级以及以 -er，-ow 结尾的形容词在词尾加-er；以 y 结尾的形容词在词尾去 y 加-ier；以 e 结尾的形容词在词尾直接加-r 构成。

例：dark → darker；quick → quicker；early → earlier；clever → cleverer；simple → simpler；narrow→narrower

2．多音节形容词的比较级在其前加 more 构成。

例：important→more important；beautiful→more beautiful

3．表语形容词以及由分词变来的形容词，在其前加 more 构成。

例：afraid →more afraid；interesting→more interesting；pleased→more pleased

4．少数形容词的比较级是不规则的。

例：good→better；bad→worse；far→farther / further

• 比较级的基本用法：

1．原级比较

1）由"... as＋形容词＋as ..."或"... as＋形容词＋名词＋as ..."构成。

例句：My old mobile phone is as good as your new one.

The newly designed iPad can download as much information as the computer does.

2）由"... not so（as）＋形容词＋as ..."或"... not so（as）＋形容词＋名词＋as ..."构成。

例句：Luckily the new machine was not so heavy as it was before.

2．不同级比较

1）由"...形容词比较级＋than ..."构成。

例句：The gift my parents gave me was more important than the other presents.

2）由"... many / much more＋可数/不可数名词＋than ..."构成。

例句：The new TV can get much more programs than before.

• 比较级的特殊用法：

1．"比较级＋ and＋比较级"或"more and more / less and less＋原级"结构表示"越来越……"的意思，与这类结构搭配的常用动词有 grow，get，become 等。

例句：She felt herself becoming more and more nervous.

As the winter is drawing near，it's getting colder and colder.

2. the＋比较级＋of the two＋名词。

例句：Jane is the taller of the two children in our family.

3. "the＋比较级...，the＋比较级..."，表示"越……，越……"。

例句：The more magazines you sell，the more money you will get.

4. "否定＋比较级"相当于最高级。

例句：— Wait until we get a satisfactory reply，will you?

— I couldn't agree more. The idea sounds great to me.

5. "a＋比较级＋名词(than ...)"结构常出现在以 never 构成的完成时态的动词后面。

例句：How beautifully she sings! I have never heard a better voice.

6. 倍数表示法：... times as＋形容词原级＋as ...；... times＋形容词比较级＋than ...；... times the＋性质名词＋of ...。

例句：The dining hall is three times as large as that one.

The dining hall is three times larger than that one.

The dining hall is three times the size of that one.

练习　单项选择

1. The new group of students is better-behaved than the other group who stayed here _____.

　　A. early　　　　　　B. earlier　　　　　C. earliest　　　　D. the earliest

2. Of the two coats，I'd choose the _____ one to spare some money for a book.

　　A. cheapest　　　　　　　　　　　B. cheaper

　　C. more expensive　　　　　　　　D. most expensive

3. There is an old proverb，"Love me，love my dog. " But there is _____ wisdom in this："Love me，love my book."

　　A. some　　　　　　B. much　　　　　　C. more　　　　　D. most

4. With April 18's railway speedup，highway and air transport will have to compete with _____ service for passengers.

　　A. good　　　　　　B. better　　　　　C. best　　　　　D. the best

5. The melon the Smiths served at dinner would have tasted _____ if it had been put in the fridge for a little while.

　　A. good　　　　　　B. better　　　　　C. best　　　　　D. well

6. Speaking of all the songs he has written，I think this is probably his _____ one.

　　A. better-known　　　　B. well-known　　　C. best-known　　D. most-known

7. After two years' research，we now have a _____ better understanding of the disease.

　　A. very　　　　　　B. far　　　　　C. fairly　　　　D. quite

8. Work gets done _____ when people do it together，and the rewards are higher too.

    A. easily　　　　　　B. very easy　　　　C. more easily　　　D. easier

9. Your story is perfect. I've never heard _____ before.

    A. the better one　　B. the best one　　　C. a better one　　　D. a good one

10. This washing machine is environmentally friendly because it uses _____ water and electricity than _____ models.

    A. less，older　　　　B. less，elder　　　C. fewer，older　　　D. fewer，elder

表达物品的重要性及发表感受的高分细节：

> 1）正确运用条件句强调事物的重要性。如：If human beings didn't have paper，they wouldn't be able to pass the culture to next generation.
>
> 2）正确使用描述对物品喜爱的词汇。如：The kite makes me feel nostalgic about the fun I had with grandpa.

下面我们针对以上两个高分细节进行解析：

高分细节一：正确运用第二和第三条件句强调事物的重要性

首先我们来看一个实例：

Student：... If I had to organize trips out with my friends a few days in advance or contact friends who live far away by letter，life just wouldn't be as much fun ...

从上述例子可以发现，第二、第三条件句是我们在雅思口语考试中推荐考生采用的一种强调物品重要性的方式。这样的表述更加生动具体，口语语言感更强。在前面的课程中我们学习了第三条件句，接下来我们来分析第二条件句的结构和用法。

第二条件句是非真实条件句的一种，它表示现在或将来不可能实现，或实现的可能性很小的一种假设。它的谓语动词所表示的动作、状态都是虚构的、假想的、不可能实现或实现的可能性很小的。第二条件句的结构为：

1. if＋动词过去式，would（n't）＋动词原形

例句：If I didn't have a laptop，I wouldn't be able to study English online.

If everyone in the country knew first aid，many lives would be saved.

2. would（n't）＋动词原形＋if＋动词过去式

例句：I wouldn't be able to study English online if I didn't have a laptop.

Many lives would be saved if everyone in the country knew first aid.

备注：if 条件句中如有 were，should，had，可以省去 if，并使用倒装语序。

例句：Were I a boy，I would join the army.

在 if 非真实条件状语从句中的谓语动词如果是 be，其过去形式一般用 were。

练习　请用第二条件句造句

1. _____

2. _____

3. _____

4. _____

5. _____

高分细节二：正确使用描述对物体感受的表达方式

首先我们来看两个实例：

Student：... whenever I see the photograph I took with my grandparents I always start feeling warm ...

Student：... I am quite sentimental about my father's watch, which is why I've kept for so many years even though it's really old ...

从以上两个例子可以发现，在描述物品时会需要一些表达我们对某物的感受的表达方式。而大部分的考生在表达感受的过程中比较单一地使用 important，like 这样的单词。接下来补充一些表达感受的单词和短语。

1. 表达实际感受的词语：

inspired / intrigued / fascinated / delighted / thrilled / exhilarated / relieved / relaxed / sentimental（about）/ enthusiastic（about）/ nostalgic

2. 提出感受的表达方式：

- （it）makes me feel ...

- （it）makes me think about / of ...

- （it）reminds me of ...

- （it）'s important to me because ...

- whenever I（do something）I feel ...

- I couldn't bear to part with ...

例句：My new mobile phone makes me feel delighted.

I couldn't bear to part with my newly bought iPad — it makes me think about the money I saved for so long.

复习物品类话题描述结构：

物品类话题描述结构：

Step 1：Say what it is and where did you get it（who did you get it from）

第一步：描述它是什么，你从哪里或者从谁那里得到它的

Step 2：Say what it looks like and what is its function

第二步：描述它的外观和功能是什么

Step 3：Say how is it

第三步：评价它到底怎么样

Step 4: Say why it is special and how you feel about it

第四步:描述为什么它很特殊以及你对它的感受

请结合下面的考题将描述结构以及所解析的高分细节进行认真的练习

真题例举:

1. Describe a photograph that is memorable to you

   You should mention: who were in the photo

   where and when it was taken

   where it was now and why it was memorable and important to you

2. Describe a thing you lost

   You should say: when and where you lost it

   what you were doing at that time

   what kind of inconvenience the loss caused you and how you overcame it

3. Describe a website that has influenced you

   You should mention: how you found it

   why you use it and what you do when you visit the website

4. Describe a movie you watched lately

   You should mention: what is the movie and where you watched it

   what is this movie about and how you feel about it

5. Describe a machine that is important in your life

   You should say: what it is

   why it is important to you and how this machine has influence your life

第四节　事件类话题

在本节中,我们将通过对事件类话题描述结构的讲解以及运用让同学们学会如何在雅思口语考试中描述一件事情。

首先我们来看一些地点类的真题:(提示小题省略)

• Describe a birthday party you attended
• Describe a game you played when you were a child
• Describe an unforgettable success in your life
• Describe the weekend you spent last week

描述结构步骤:在解答事件类话题过程中,考生可以按照以下结构步骤进行陈述:

Step 1：Say what it was and when it happened
步骤1:介绍事情是什么及发生的时间

Step 2：Say where it happened and who was there
步骤2:介绍事件是在什么地方发生的,在场的有谁

Step 3：Say what happened and why it happened
步骤3:介绍发生了什么和发生的原因

Step 4：Say why this event is special and how you felt about it
步骤4:介绍这个事件有什么特殊的或者你对这个事件的感受是什么

答案范例解析:我们通过样题一作为例子来解析如何根据描述结构完成陈述

题一:Describe a positive experience in your childhood

You should say：when it happened

where it happened

whom you were with and explain why it was positive

Interviewer：Tell me about a positive experience in your childhood

Step 1：Say what it was and when it happened

Student：I clearly remember a positive experience in my childhood was participating in a speech contest. It was an unforgettable experience in my life. I was just eight years old at that time.

Step 2：Say where it happened and who was there

Student：Our school was going to hold a speech contest，and every class had to pick five students to take part in the contest. My class had already chosen five members.

Step 3：Say what happened and why it happened

Student：But on that day of the speech contest，one of them was sick and could not join in. Our Chinese teacher was very worried and asked one student to replace that sick student. There was nobody who wanted to accept it. Though I was very timid at that time，after several minute's thought，I determined to have a try. Finally I got the second prize in the same group and was praised by my teacher.

Step 4：Say why this event is special and how you felt about it

Student：After this experience I began to realize the meaning of "Where there is a will，there is a way." I think I succeed due to my courage and confidence. If I didn't apply for this chance，I wouldn't have achieved this successful experience.

介绍事件的高分细节：

1）正确介绍事件的名称。如：I was lucky enough to attend The Olympic Games in Beijing 2008 . . .

2）正确运用时间和表示时间的短语。如：A while ago I went to pick up the gift I left in the shop . . .

3）正确运用过去进行时、一般过去时和过去完成时设定事件场景。如：It was a basketball competition held when I was in the university about 3 years ago.

下面将针对以上高分细节来进行说明。

高分细节一：正确介绍事件的名称

首先我们来看几个例子：

Student ：I clearly remember the day I won the second prize in the calligraphy contest in my school . . .

Student：When I was a child，I usually played a game named "the eagle preys on the chicken" which was popular at that time . . .

从以上两个例子中我们可以看出，要描述一件事情首先将事情的名称正确地进行介绍是必不可少的。这成了在描述事件过程中最初步的要求。接下来介绍一下常见的生活中一些事件的名称。

事件名称：

●School event：class / activity / exercise / role-play / summer camp / English corner / class-discussion / debate

●Journey：school trip / education trip / road trip / day trip / holiday / vacation / tour

● Competition：sports match / basketball match / sports competition / chess competition speech contest / the Olympic Games / the Asian Games

●Party：birthday party / farewell party / house-warming party / hen party / stag party / ball party

备注：我们经常会用以下两种句式结构来介绍事件。

1. It is＋the time（that／when）＋did something.

例句：It is the time when I went on a day trip ...

It is the time that I attended a farewell party ...

2. It is＋the first time＋did something.

例句：It is the first time I attended a formal ball.

It is the first time I played golf.

练习　选词填空

sports match　holiday　exercise　debate　speech　contest　farewell party

1. My girlfriend and I went to Rome for a _____ and I proposed to her.
2. The topic I used in the _____ is about King Arthur.
3. The most exciting _____ I ever watched is the NBA championships.
4. All of my friends attended my _____ before I went to England.
5. Our team beat the Qinghua University's in a _____.

高分细节二：正确运用时间和表示时间的短语

首先我们来看几个例子：

Student：I want to talk about one interesting experience I had when I was a child ...

Student：The party I would like to talk about is the one on the 5th of November，2005

...

从以上两个例子中我们可以看出，在描述事件的过程中时间是一个非常重要的因素。但是在中国考生描述事件发生时间的过程中会存在大量的介词错误。介词的运用是衡量一个考生英语程度非常重要的标准，所以需要引起考生的注意。接下来我们就来解析一下能和时间短语搭配的介词以及时间的表示方法。

表示具体时间：

• In（months，seasons，years，noons，long periods of time）

例：in November／in spring／in 1999／in the evening／in the last 15 years

• On（days，special days）

例：on the 6th of December 2010／on my parent's 25th wedding anniversary

• At（specific times，noons，midnights，festivals）

例：at 12 o'clock／at noon／at Chinese New Year

• During（months，seasons，festivals，long periods of time）

例：during November／during the winter／during the Spring Festival／during this 5 months

表示不确定时间：

• Around（times，months，occasions，festivals，special day）

例：around February／around 1 o'clock／around my graduation／around Christmas

• Once

例：Once I went to the supermarket to . . .

　• A few years / months / long periods of time ago

例：A while ago，I found my lost watch.

　• When

例：I went on a trip when I was in the university.

练习　单项选择

1. Children get gifts _____ Christmas and _____ their birthdays.
   A. on, on　　　　　B. at, on　　　　　C. in, in　　　　　D. in, on

2. A lot of students in our school were born _____ March，1981.
   A. in　　　　　B. at　　　　　C. on　　　　　D. since

3. Tim suddenly returned _____ a rainy night.
   A. on　　　　　B. at　　　　　C. in　　　　　D. during

4. My grandfather was born _____ Oct. 10，1935.
   A. on　　　　　B. in　　　　　C. at　　　　　D. of

5. The train is starting _____ five minutes.
   A. in　　　　　B. at　　　　　C. for　　　　　D. still

6. Mike does his exercises _____ seven _____ the evening.
   A. on, to　　　　　B. at, in　　　　　C. by, of　　　　　D. at, on

7. The population of the world has grown very fast _____ four hundred years.
   A. for the past　　　B. in the pass　　　C. in the past　　　D. for past

8. We returned to our hometown _____ .
   A. next week　　　B. in the last week　　C. last week　　　D. for a week

9. Great changes have taken place _____ .
   A. in the last few year　　　　　B. in the last few years
   C. last year　　　　　D. on the last year

10. Children wake up very early _____ the morning of Christmas Day.
    A. in　　　　　B. on　　　　　C. for　　　　　D. at

高分细节三：使用一般过去时、过去进行时和过去完成时描述事件

首先我们来看几个例子：

Student：. . . when the game was playing，I would often discuss it with some of my friends . . .

Student：I'd like to talk about the time that I was late for an exam. It was in my last year at secondary school，when I was taking my final exam . . .

在雅思口语考试中，通常要求考生描述的事件为已经发生过的事情，在这时候就要求考生能够正确地运用时态去描述发生在过去的事情。接下来我们来分析一下描述过

去发生事情的时态。

一般过去时和过去进行时:在一个句子中同时出现一般过去时和过去进行时,那么不可延续动作发生在可延续的动作中。句子结构为:

- (while / when)＋was / were＋verb-ing（when)＋past verb

例句：While I was studying at university，I heard an interesting story.

I was studying at university when I heard an interesting story.

- past verb（while / when)＋was / were＋verb-ing

例句：I heard an interesting story while I was studying at university.

一般过去时与过去完成时:在一个句子中同时出现一般过去时和过去完成时,那么先发生的动作用过去完成时,后发生的动作用一般过去时。句子结构为:

- had＋past participle（动词的过去分词）＋past verb

例句：I had studied at university for a few months before my teacher told me . . .

Because I had worked really well in the company，the manager promoted me.

- past verb＋had＋past participle

例句：The manager promoted me because I had worked really well in the company.

练习：用正确的动词时态填空

1. It was warm，so I _____(take) off my coat.

2. Jane _____(wait) for me when I _____(arrive).

3. Sue wasn't hungry，so she _____(eat) anything.

4. My brother came into the bedroom while I _____(dance).

5. When I arrived at his office, he _____(speak) on the phone.

6. Paul _____(go) out with Jane after he _____(make) a phone call.

7. Tom _____(say) he _____(read) the book twice.

8. Our plan _____(fail) because we _____(make) a bad mistake.

9. When the chairman _____(finish) speaking, he _____(leave) the hall.

10. The Reads were _____(have) lunch when I _____(get) to their house.

描述事件发生原因和地点的高分细节：

> 1) 正确运用被动语态描述事件发生的原因。如:... The speech contest was organized by our student union . . .
>
> 2) 正确运用地点介词表示事件发生的场所。如:There were many trees along the river bank.

下面将针对以上高分细节来进行说明。

高分细节一:正确运用被动语态描述事件发生的原因

首先我们来看几个例子:

Student：... The basketball match was broadcasted by CCTV5 and that is the best game I have ever seen ...

Student：... my plane ticket to UK was bought for me by my parents. That's how the story began ...

从以上两个例子中可以发现,在描述事件发生原因的过程中被动语态是一种常用的表达方式。我们在前文中已经给大家介绍了被动语态在物品类话题中的运用,接下来我们来结合事件类话题复习一下被动语态。

被动语态在各个时态中的句型结构：

• 一般现在时 is / are＋past participle

例句：The TV program is broadcasted by CCTV.

• 一般将来时 will be＋past participle

例句：The contest will be held in our stadium.

• 现在进行时 is / are＋being＋past participle

例句：The building is being built by that company.

• 一般过去时 was / were＋past participle

例句：The picture was taken in Shanghai with my family.

• 现在完成时 have / has＋been＋past participle

例句：Our task has already been done by Alex.

• 过去完成时 had＋been＋past participle

例句：The ticket had been bought by my parents before I went to the airport.

• 过去进行时 was / were＋being＋past participle

例句：The speech was being prepared by our group when the teacher came.

• 情态动词 情态动词＋be＋past participle

例句：All the goods must be sold out by now.

练习：用正确的动词形式填空

Ted Robinson has been worried all the week. Last Tuesday, he _____ (receive) a letter from the police station. In the letter he _____ (ask) to call at the station. Ted didn't know why he _____ (want) by the police, but he _____ (go) to the station yesterday and now he _____ (not, worry) any more. At the station he _____ (tell) by a smiling policeman that his bicycle _____ (find). Five days ago, the policeman _____ (tell) him, the bicycle _____ (pick) up in a small village four hundred miles ways. Now it _____ (send) to his home on the way by train. Ted _____ (surprise) when he _____ (hear) the news. He was amused too, because he never thought that the bicycle _____ (can, find) again. It _____ (take) away by someone twenty years ago when he _____ (be) a boy of fifteen!

高分细节二:正确使用地点介词描述事件发生的地点

首先让我们来看几个例子:

Student: ... A great journey I had a few years ago was when my girlfriend and I flew in a helicopter over the Grand Canyon in the USA ...

Student: ... Last year I went to Yunnan and visited the Stone Forest just outside of Kunming ...

从上面两个例子可以发现,在描述事件发生地点的时候我们需要运用地点介词。接下来我们来介绍一些常见的地点介词:

- In+ enclosing or larger place

in the countryside / in the middle of nowhere

- At+ specific place or location

at the top of the mountain / at the end of the street

- On+ a surface or roads

on the fifth floor / on a main road

- Over / above+ a certain place or location

above a Japanese restaurant / the flag flies over Tian'anmen Square

- Next to / beside / by+ a certain place or location

by the seaside / next to the shop / beside the lake

- Opposite / across from+ a certain place

I work opposite the city library.

The place we held our match is just across from the square.

- In front of+ a certain place

The Bund in Shanghai is just in front of the main historical building.

- Far from

I live far from the city center.

练习:选词填空

1. Taiwan is _____ the southeast of China. (in, on, to)
2. Go _____ the bridge _____ the river, you'll find the shop. (across, through; over, above)
3. I came _____ an old friend in the park this afternoon and we talked for a long time. (at, by, across, into)
4. There is a bookstore _____ the other side of the street. (in, on, at)
5. There is no hole _____ the wall. (in, on, over, at)
6. We lay down _____ a tree to rest. (under, over, above, below)
7. There is a railway _____ these two cities. (in, among, between, at)

描述事件发生经过的高分细节：

> 1）正确运用直接引语与间接引语。如：He said I would never make it. / She said，"You are the best among all the others."
>
> 2）正确运用表示顺序的表达方式描述经过。如：Shortly afterwards he came running back ...

下面针对以上高分细节来进行说明。

高分细节一：正确运用直接引语与间接引语

首先来看一个例子：

Student：... In the conversation I had with my dad I had a lot of helpful ideas to help me with my decision. He told me I am an adult now I need think about the responsibility before I do anything ...

在上面这个例子中，考生运用了间接引语来描述事情当中的对话。直接引语与间接引语是引用别人说话的两种方式，一种是讲述别人的原话，并把它放在引号里，这叫直接引语；另一种是用自己的话来转述别人，并且不能用引号，这就是间接引语。接下来我们分析一下直接引语与间接引语的用法。

直接引语变间接引语的五点变化：

1. 时态变化

直接引语	间接引语
一般现在时	一般过去时
一般过去时	过去完成时
一般过去时	过去将来时
现在进行时	过去进行时
过去完成时	过去完成时
过去进行时	过去进行时
can	could
may	might
must	must / had to

例句："I like English very much," he said. →He said that he liked English very much.

He said，"It would rain soon." →He said that it would rain soon.

备注：1）如果直接引语为客观真理，则变为间接引语时时态不变：

The teacher said to us，"Knowledge is power."

The teacher told us that knowledge is power.

2）有时由于直接引语有特定的过去时态状语，变为间接引语时时态也可不变：He said，"My daughter was born in 1997."

He said that his daughter was born in 1997.

2. 时间状语、地点状语、指示代词和动词的变化

	直接引语	间接引语
时间状语	now	then
时间状语	today	that day
时间状语	tonight	that night
时间状语	this week	that week
时间状语	yesterday	the day before
时间状语	the day before yesterday	two days before
时间状语	two days ago	three days before
时间状语	last week	the last week
时间状语	tomorrow	the next day
时间状语	next week	the next week
指示代词	this	that
指示代词	these	those
地点状语	here	there
动词	come	go

例句：1）He said，"I'm sleeping now."

→ He said that he was sleeping then.

2）She said，"My sister doesn't want to come here."

→She said that her sister didn't want to go there.

3. 当直接引语为一般疑问句时，变间接引语的方法：将直接引语变为由 if 或 whether 引导的宾语从句跟在叙述动词之后。

例句："Is everybody here?" the teacher asked.

The teacher asked if / whether everybody was there.

4. 当直接引语为特殊疑问句时，变为间接引语的方法是：将直接引语变为由"疑问词"引导的宾语从句，跟在引述之后。

例句：She asked，"Where does he live?"

She asked where he lived.

5. 当直接引语为祈使句时，变为间接引语的方法是：使用 ask / tell / order sb. to do sth. 这一结构进行转换，若祈使句为否定式则用 ask / tell / order sb. not to do sth. 其中 ask，tell，order 的选择要根据句子的语气而定。

例句："Get up early tomorrow，Bill."he said.

He told Bill to get up early the next day.

练习：将所给直接引语变为间接引语，每空一词

1. "I never eat meat." he said.

   He said that _____ never _____ meat.

2. "I've found my wallet." he said to me.

   He _____ me that he _____ _____ _____ wallet.

3. "I took it home with me." she said.

   She said that _____ _____ _____ it home with her.

4. The teacher said，"The sun rises in the east and goes down in the west."

   The teacher said that the sun _____ in the east and _____ down in the west.

5. "I met her yesterday." he said to me.

   He _____ me that he _____ met her the day _____.

高分细节二：正确运用表示顺序的表达方式描述经过

首先我们来看一个例子：

Student：... I remember studying by myself in my bedroom and feeling exhausted. I'm not really sure what happen next，but I must have fallen asleep when I was studying because the next thing I knew it was the next day and the sunlight was streaming through the window. Straight away，I started panicking as it felt very late. Looking at my watch, I found that I was already 20 minutes late for my exam ...

　　从上面的例子中可以发现，为了更好地描述事件的先后发展顺序，我们在描述过程中往往需要一些用来提示顺序的表达方式。接下来我们来介绍一些该表达方式：

- To start with / at the beginning / at first
- As soon as / immediately / straight away
- By the time that / then
- Afterwards / following that / after / soon after / shortly after
- In the end / finally

例句：

　　1. To start with I felt very nervous after the exam but shortly after I felt much more relaxed.

　　2. As soon as we entered the stadium we realized that we were very early.

　　3. I watched a movie directed by him a few years ago. Following that I hope to be a man like him.

练习:用下列词组造句

1) to start with

_____

2) straight away

_____

3) by the time that

_____

4) afterwards

_____

5) in the end

_____

描述对事件感受的高分细节:

> 1) 正确使用描述事件和感觉的形容词。如:This event was important to me because ... / I felt regret whenever I think of those times.
>
> 2) 正确使用虚拟语气表达事件的重要性。如:If I hadn't participated in the competition, I wouldn't have had the confidence.
>
> 3) 选择适当的表达方式结束话题。如:I wish I hadn't done it, I still feel stupid every time I think about it.

下面将针对以上高分细节来进行说明。

高分细节一:正确使用描述事件和感觉的形容词

首先我们来看一个例子:

Student: Needless to say this was a pretty horrible experience for me to go through. Apart from feeling so anxious on the day, I was also worried sick about what consequence I was going to take ...

从上面的例子中可以发现,当我们在评价事件的特殊性和影响时,需要有一些适当的形容词来修饰句子。而考生容易出现的不足就是缺乏这样的形容词而导致描述中词汇单一重复。接下来我们来介绍一些在事件类话题中常用的形容词:

◉Interesting:funny / amusing / fascinating / curious / stimulating / enlightening

◉Strange:unusual / bizarre / weird / mysterious / peculiar / random / crazy / wild

◉Surprising :amazing / astonishing / astounding / awe-inspiring / incredible / breathtaking

◉Good:inspiring / life-changing / enjoyable / wonderful / important / refreshing / encouraging / moving

◉ Bad:horrible / terrible / awful / depressing / unpleasant / frustrating / disappointing / embarrassing

高分细节二：正确使用虚拟语气表达事件的重要性

首先我们来看一个例子：

Student：... I probably wouldn't choose movie for my major if our school hadn't invited Zhang Yimou to give us a speech ...

从上面这个例子中可以发现,虚拟语气用来表示事件的重要性可以起到强调和加重语义的作用。而虚拟语气在英语语法中属于重点难点语法环节,很多考生在考试的时候没有把握不敢应用。接下来我们来解析一下虚拟语气的用法。

虚拟语气用法及动词形式：

1) 表示与现在事实相反的情况：

从句：主语＋过去时　　　主句：主语＋should / would / could / might＋do

例：If I were you, I would take an umbrella.

If I knew his telephone number, I would tell you.

2) 表示与过去事实相反的情况

从句：主语＋had done　　　主句：主语＋should / would / could / might＋have done

例：If I had got there earlier, I should / could have met her.

If he had taken my advice, he would not have made such a mistake.

3) 表示对将来情况的主观推测

从句：①if＋主语＋were to do　　　主句：①主语＋should / would / could / might＋do

②if＋主语＋did / were　　　②主语＋should / would / could / might＋do

③if＋主语＋should＋do　　　③主语＋should / would / could / might＋do

例：If he should come here tomorrow, I should / would talk to him.

If there were a heavy snow next Sunday, we would not go skating.

If she were to be there next Monday, I would tell her about the matter.

4) 有时候,虚拟条件句中,结果主句和条件从句的谓语动作若不是同时发生时,虚拟语气的形式应作相应的调整。

①从句的动作与过去事实相反,主句的动作与现在或现在正在发生的事实不符。

例：If I had worked hard at school, I would be an engineer, too.

If they had informed us, we would not come here now.

②从句的动作与现在事实相反,而主句的动作与过去事实不符。

例：If he were free today, we would have sent him to Beijing.

If he knew her, he would have greeted her.

5) 当虚拟条件句的谓语动词含有 were, should, had 时,if 可以省略,这时条件从句要用倒装语序,即将 were, should, had 等词置于句首,这种多用于书面语。

例：Should he agree to go there, we would send him there.

Were she here, she would agree with us.

6) 非真实条件句中的条件从句有时不表达出来,只暗含在副词、介词短语、上下文或其他方式中表示出来,这种句子叫做含蓄条件句,在多数情况下,条件会暗含在短语中,如 without ..., but for ... 等。

例:But for his help, we would be working now.

Without your instruction, I would not have made such great progress.

7) 有时候,在虚拟条件句中,主、从句可以省略其中的一个,来表示说话人的一种强烈的感情。

①省略从句

例:He would have finished it.

You could have passed this exam.

②省略主句

例:If I were at home now.

If only I had got it.

练习:单项选择

1. He treated me as if _____ his own son.

    A. I am   B. I would be   C. I was   D. I were

2. A few minutes earlier and we _____ the rain.

    A. have caught   B. had caught

    C. could have caught   D. were to catch

3. I'm glad I went over all my notes; otherwise _____.

    A. I may have failed   B. I'd fail

    C. I'd have failed   D. I'll have failed

4. What should we do if it _____ tomorrow?

    A. should snow   B. would snow   C. snow   D. will snow

5. If only I _____ my watch!

    A. hadn't lost   B. haven't lost   C. didn't lost   D. don't lose

6. You _____ such a serious mistake if you had followed his advice.

    A. may not make   B. might not make

    C. shouldn't have made   D. might not have made

7. We _____ the work on time without your help.

    A. hadn't had finished   B. didn't have finished

    C. couldn't have finished   D. can't have finished

8. If it were not for the fact that you _____ ill, I would ask you to do this right now.

    A. were   B. had been   C. are   D. being

高分细节三:选择适当的表达方式结束话题

首先我们来看一个例子:

Student: ... This event taught me the importance of not being late — I've always been punctual ever since!

上面这个例子中,考生用了一个感叹句型既说明了事情的重要性以及特殊性同时也以恰当的方式结束了话题。接下来我们来介绍一些常用的话题结束方式。

• The . . . taught me that . . .

例句:The meeting taught me that we all should learn how to work in a group and how to do work in a team effectively.

• The . . . was important to / for me because . . .

例句:The conversation was important to me because I felt the love from my family.

• Through this experience I learnt the importance of . . .

例句:Through this experience I learnt the importance of being honest.

• I will never forget . . .

• 例句: I will never forgot the time I spent with Director Zhang Yimou because it was inspiring.

• Overall, it was a rewarding experience and I learned a lot . . .

例句: Overall, it was a rewarding experience and I learned a lot about how to make designs.

• I would love to do it again if I had the chance . . .

例句:I would love to do it again if I had the chance — it was amazing.

• Although I enjoyed it at the time, I wouldn't want to do it again because . . .

例句:Although I enjoyed it at the time, I wouldn't want to do it again because I don't think it will be as much fun as the first time.

• In the future I will . . .

例句:In the future I will practice the knowledge I learned from this experience and try to be a better person in order to make the world better.

在事件类话题的最后我们再次来复习下一答题的结构:

Step 1: Say what it was and when it happened

步骤1:介绍事情是什么及发生的时间

Step 2: Say where it happened and who was there

步骤2:介绍事件是在什么地方发生的,在场的有谁

Step 3: Say what happened and why it happened

步骤3:介绍发生了什么和发生的原因

Step 4: Say why this event is special and how you felt about it

步骤4:介绍这个事件有什么特殊或者你对这个事件的感受是什么

请考生在按照结构回答的同时将我们在书中所解析以及练习的高分语言细节运用在考题之内,这样能帮助考生尽可能地达到想要的分数。下列考试真题请认真练习:

1. Describe an important conversation you had in your life

You should mention: When and where did this conversation happened

Who did you have conversation with

What it is about and explain why you think it is important to you

2. Describe an important decision you made

You should mention: What it was

When you made it and why you made this decision

3. Describe a special or unusual thing you did recently

You should mention: What it was

Where it happened and whom you were with

4. Describe a traffic jam you met

You should mention: When and where it happened

Whom you were wait and how you felt about it

第六章　雅思口语第三部分——深入讨论

雅思口语考试第三部分介绍

雅思口语考试第三部分的考试时间为 4 到 5 分钟,考官将对一些比较广泛的社会问题与考生进行双向讨论。考生需要清晰地表达并论证自己的观点,同时向考官展示出自己能够运用英语母语者的思维讨论问题的技巧,并就一些不太熟悉的话题进行广泛而深入的讨论。

第三部分高分公式介绍

第三部分的常见题型可以归纳为 3 大类别:主观意见陈述题、优缺点表述题、问题解决题。

第一节　主观意见陈述题

1) 真题样题:

Do you think money equals with happiness?
Do you think electronic games are good for children?
Do you think that men and women have the same requirements for life?

从以上例题中可以发现,在口语考试第三类的问题中,问题本身都是具有高度争议性的题目。这样的题目没有所谓的正确答案,考生可以对问题持任意符合一定逻辑常识的观点。题目主要考查的是考生在回答中对于观点的表达以及用语言论证观点能力。

2) 答题结构:

结合第三部分的考试要求,在回答的时候最好采用在第一部分所运用的回答结构来完成即"TSC"结构:

T:topic sentence(开场句即主旨句,在开头陈述自己的所持有的观点)
S:supporting details(支持细节,运用个人经验、例子、数据等具体信息来证明观点)
C:conclusion(结论/可选择)

3) 答案范例解析:

Interviewer:Do you think electronic games are good for children?

T：topic sentence

Student：Yes，maybe people think that electronic games are bad for children. But in my opinion, electronic games should be considered as another form of entertainment.

S：supporting details

Student：And most electronic games involve letters, numbers and patterns which can foster the children's identification ability. While playing, they can also exercise their reaction capacity. Besides, they often need cooperation to finish a game, so this will develop their team-spirit.

C：conclusion

Student：As far as I concern, during the procedure of playing electronic games children will obtain many abilities other than fun.

4) 主观意见陈述题高分细节：

> （1）正确地表达观点，如：Yes, I think that children in middle school and high school should wear a uniform to school.
> （2）正确地运用表达论证观点的方式，如：I strongly believe it is essential for helping the old people find their position in the society.
> （3）运用多样的论证方式。

下面将针对以上高分细节来进行说明

高分细节一：正确地表达观点

首先来看两个例子：

Interviewer：Do you believe people should pay to enter public parks?

Student：No, absolutely not! The way I see it, all public parks should be free for everyone ...

Interviewer：Do you think that vegetables are important part of a diet?

Student：Sure, I think that they give people a lot of vitamins.

从以上两个例子中可以发现，在回答问题的开头考生通常需要对问题提出一个观点。在考试中很多考生在表达观点的方式相对单一，如"I think ..." "In my opinion"这样的回答多次反复出现，从而影响了回答的质量。接下来将介绍一些常用的表达观点的方式：

①表达同意或者不同意的方式：

Yes, I do.

Sure.

Certainly（not）.

Not really.

Absolutely（not）.

I'm not sure agree.

②介绍具体想法和观点的方式

In my opinion，...

In my point of view，...

As far as I am concerned，...

As for me，...

From where I stand...

I'd like to point out that...

It seems to me that...

What I reckon is ...

Frankly speaking，...

To be honest，...

Actually...

Personally，...

To tell the truth ...

I agree with ...

It depends, different people have different ...

It is difficult for me to make a choice（tell the differences），you know ...（on one hand ... on the other hand ... ）

Well，it is an interesting / tough question，because...

I am not much of a ... ，so I know little about ... but I guess ...

高分细节二：正确地运用表达论证观点的方式

首先来看两个例子：

Student：... I strongly believe that it is essential for giving children a sense of identity and unity because ...

Student：... I feel that it would be inappropriate to deny people healthcare just because they are poor, for example...

　　从以上两个例子中可以发现,在讨论问题的过程中考生会针对问题发表肯定的或者是否定的观点,并通过解释原因或者举例子等方式来论证观点的正确性。所以如何发表肯定或者否定的观点以及论证观点的方式至关重要：

①表达肯定观点：

It's good / important for + verb-ing

例句：It is good for giving old generation enough attention.

It's essential / vital for + verb-ing

例句：It is essential for taking the situation into consideration.

It gives us the opportunity / freedom to + verb

例句：Public transportation gives us the opportunity to stop using private vehicles.

②表示否定的观点：

◉It would be inappropriate to verb

例句：It would be inappropriate to let children watch all kinds of TV programs.

◉It could have a bad effect on ...

例句：It could have a bad effect on the society.

◉It's not good for society if people...

例句：It is not good for society if people lost faith in their government.

◉It's unethical to verb ...

例句：It's unethical to expose people's privacy without permission.

高分细节三：运用多样的论证方式

①表示原因

Because(of) ...	Since ...
As ...	Due to ... , ...
We attribute ... to ...	We owe ... to ...
Thanks to ...	Now that ...
On account of ...	... leads to ...
... is responsible for ...	... results in ...

②举例说明

Let me give you an example.	to make it clear to you, ...
take ... for instance ...	such as ...
In other words ...	in this case ...
By way of illustration	

③增补递近

In addition ...	further more ...

Besides . . .	more over . . .
What's more . . .	similarly, . . .

④强调肯定

certainly, . . .	above all, . . .
indeed . . .	of course, . . .
surely, . . .	actually, . . .
as a matter of fact, . . .	chiefly, . . .
especially, . . .	primarily, . . .
in particular, . . .	undoubtedly, . . .
absolutely, . . .	most importantly, . . .

⑤归纳总结

to sum up, . . .	to conclude, . . .
in a word, . . .	in short, . . .
in brief, . . .	all in all, . . .
in all, . . .	to put it in a nutshell, . . .
in summary	

5）真题范例：

Q：What do you think of the transportation system in the city you've visited?

A：I was thoroughly impressed. Compared with some other cities that I've seen, the buses were cheap and clean. While they're still crowded, enough buses run on each route to allow passengers to arrive at their destinations on time in a certain degree of comfort. Road congestion is kept to a minimum. The bicycle lanes are well regulated and sufficiently wide, and the facilities of pedestrians are well-regulated to avoid unnecessary accidents.

Q：Do you think people should pay for entering those places for daily leisure? Why?

A：Applying a modest fee to those who actually make use of such places is not unreasonable. Such places have been equipped with facilities for entertainment and enjoyment, and as time goes by, the infrastructure, especially the park facilities vulnerable to weather damage and extensive daily use, will become broken-down and require replacement. To purchase and maintain these facilities may cost a considerable amount of money. In light of how spiritedly people use these facilities, compared to, say, a public museum, it would appear reasonable to request of them some form of basic maintenance fee.

Q：Should the facilities be opened to society?

A: In my opinion, the facilities should not be opened to all the members in our society. First, it is not equal to those students. For students, they have studied very hard for several years until they enter the holy place. At the same time, they pay expensive tuition fee for their education. If people are allowed to enter the campus at will, it's no doubt the quiet study environment will be disturbed. Second, the good and the bad are intermingled in the society, and no one can ensure that they will not do any harm to the facilities and members in the school. Third, without doubt, this will add great burden to school which have had enough responsibilities. In a word, the school is a holy place, and we should maintain its pureness and nobility.

Q: Do you think children should have their own rooms? Why?

A: Yes, I think so. Children's characteristics are different from adults'. They are active, imaginative and curious. Parents should pay attention to and respect their characteristics. A room of their own is a little heaven in which they can do what they want to do to satisfy their curiosity and imagination. They are often in their own world, and parents had better not interfere in their business.

Q: What qualities should a leader own?

A: Being a leader is glamorous, but the load of responsibility given to a leader is enormous. A leader must keep close communication with the masses and must be able to gain the support of his / her followers. A leader should be open to any advice or criticism and have the sense of self-cultivation. The leader's moral character is also involved. A leader must be farsighted, insist on what he / she believes and never easily give up. That's my understanding.

Q: Do you think money equals with happiness?

A: No, happiness is the most precious thing in the world while money is not.

Money can buy many things but it cannot buy happiness. So they are not equal. We can see that many people have lots of money but don't live happily; on the contrary, some people even can't get enough to eat or wear but still live a happy life.

Q: Do you think that men and women have the same requirements for life?

A: No. As long as you observe carefully, you will find that men and women have many different requirements for life. For example, men want to gain respect in life, while women want to be cherished. To men, chocolate is just another snack; but to women, it's with special meaning. Besides, men don't need three different styles of black shoes, but woman hope that shoe cabinets are full of different styles of shoes.

Q: Do you think a harmonious atmosphere is important to a company?

A: Of course. A poor working atmosphere may result in low job satisfaction, low efficiency, lack of organizational commitment and many other problem. If the staff work in an unharmonious atmosphere, they will not be able to pay full attention to their work and will feel stressful . In this case, how can the company operate well? Oppositely , a harmonious atmosphere, can make people work in a happy mood, and enable them to help each other and get along well with each other. This is beneficial for the company, too.

Q: Do you think that your notion of happiness is changing with time?

A: Yes, of course, it keeps changing at every stage in my life. When I was a child, playing with my toys and friends was happiness. When I was a student, having more free time was happiness. Now, having enough time to learn what I like seems to be the greatest happiness. In a word, in different stages, what I pursue is completely different.

Q: Do you think humor can promote interpersonal relationships?

A: Yes, of course. I think humour is a good way to promote interpersonal relationships. In the interpersonal relationships, there may be some embarrassing situations. At this time, humour is the best ideal lubricant. It also can make the boring interpersonal relationship become active. For example, while setting arguments and problems with customers, employees with a sense of humour can make solutions more acceptable for customers.

第二节　优缺点表述题

1）真题样题：

What are the advantages and disadvantages of space research?

What are the advantages and disadvantages of public transport?

What are the advantages and disadvantages of having a part-time job while at school overseas?

从以上例题中可以发现,在口语考试第三类的问题中,本类考题会要求考生列举某一观点或事物的优点以及缺点。

2）答题结构：

在这类题型中,考生往往可以选择两种思路的回答结构:一种是一面倒思路,即仅例举优点,例举两到三个优点并解释说明原因;或仅列举缺点,例举两到三个缺点并解释说明原因。另一种是相对中立思路,即例举两个优/缺点 + 一个缺/优点并解释说明原因。注意,当问题中明确要求对优点缺点都需要列举的时候则只能采用第二种思路。

3）答案范例解析：

Interviewer：What are the advantages and disadvantages of having a part-time job while at school overseas?

Main Advantage

Student：I think the main advantage of having a part time job is that it eases the financial burden which is often borne by your parents. You are able to have a little pocket money without going to your parents all the time.

Another Advantage

Student：Another advantage is that you can generally improve your English a lot if you can work part time overseas. You're working with your colleagues and they can communicate with you daily.

Disadvantage

Student：The main disadvantage is that it's tiring and the time you spend working could be spent getting good grades. Also, overseas part time work is usually not very well paid so the added pocket money may not really be worth it.

4) 优缺点表述题高分细节：

> （1）正确运用描述优点的表达方式，如：One of the main advantage of X is
> ...
>
> （2）正确运用描述缺点的表达方式，如：One principal drawback of X is ...
>
> （3）正确运用连接词和短语，如：on the one hand ... , on the other hand
> ...

下面将针对以上高分细节来进行说明

高分细节一：正确运用描述优点的表达方式

首先来看个例子：

Interviewer：What are the advantages of doing a job where you can work from home?

Student：One of the main advantage of working from home is the amount of freedom you have ... Anther good thing about it is that ...

从上面实例中可以发现在列事物优点的时候考生需要一些特定的描述方法来进行回答，而不是简单并且单调地回答 One advantage is；接下来列举一些常用描述优点的方式：

◉one of the main advantages of

◉one of the main benefits of

◉one of the major strong points of

◉the great advantage of

◉a key advantage of

◉a really good thing about

◉another good thing about

◉one more great thing about

以上表述优点的词组可以配合句型：

①Verb-ing / noun is you can ...

例句：The main advantage of cycling to work is that you can protect the environment.

②Verb-ing / noun is that you're able to ...

例句：Another key advantage of riding your bike is that it's a good form of exercise.

③ Verb-ing / noun is you don't have to

例句：One of the major strong points of eating in restaurants is you don't have to do the washing-up.

④Verb-ing / noun is you don't need to

例句：A very good thing about mobile phones is you don't need to find a place to make a contact.

高分细节二：正确运用描述缺点的表达方式

首先来看个例子：

Interviewer：What are the disadvantages of public transportation?

Student：The drawback of public transport is the wait. It's much more convenient to just jump in your car and take off.

从上面实例中可以发现在例举事物缺点的时候考生需要一些特定的描述方法来进行回答而不是简单并且单调地回答 the disadvantage is；接下来列举一些常用描述缺点的方式：

● the main disadvantages of

● one drawback of

● a / the bad thing about

● a major disadvantage of

● the one bad point about / of

● another disadvantage of

以上表述优点的词组可以配合句型：

● Verb-ing / noun is you can / might / may / could ＋ cause ... problems

● Verb-ing / noun is that it can / might/ may / could / is possible that it may

再配合以下表达方法：

● to cause problems / stress / harm to

● to get damaged / addicted to / bored with

● to not be so good for

● to have a bad impression of somebody

例句：

● The main disadvantage of working outside is that it might cause health problems in winter.

● The bad thing about owning an expensive bike is that it could get stolen.

● One drawback of being a computer programmer is that the work can be quite confusing sometimes.

● The one bad point about being outspoken and confident in class is that some people may think you are arrogant.

高分细节三：正确运用连接词和短语

首先来看个例子：

Student：... people keep fit and healthy and strong as well as being outside in the open air. On the other hand, it can be awful to work outside because you may have to work in terrible weather conditions like rain, snow and extremely cold ...

从上面实例中可以发现在回答优缺点类型题目的时候考生需要一些增加连接词和短语来联系上下文，使回答更加顺畅结构更加明晰。下面将介绍一些在该类话题中常用的连接词和短语：

◉Although
◉However
◉While
◉Yet at the same time
◉Having said that
◉Then again
◉On the one hand ... On the other hand

例句：

◉The main disadvantage of eating in restaurants is that it's expensive, although it can be exciting and fun to eat out every now and again.

◉A great thing about computers is that you can buy a computer which has state-of-the-art technology with quite low price. Then again, this means that the computer you buy now will soon be out dated.

◉The telephone is incredibly useful, while at the same time it can be quite annoying when you want to be left alone.

◉Being into fashion can be a really good thing, yet at the same time it can sometimes be a bit silly if people spend too much time thinking about fashion.

◉Going to see sports games can be fun and exciting and exhilarating. Having said that, it can be annoying to be in a crowded stadium with lots of people.

◉On the one hand contact sports are a great way to exercise, but on the other hand they can be quite dangerous.

5）真题范例：

Q：What are the advantages and disadvantages of space research?

A：I think one of the advantages is certainly that's interesting, and it feeds our knowledge about the universe. I mean, we need to know things. Also, it can be turned into a commercial enterprise. For example, many countries now sell satellites for commercial purposes and that couldn't have been achieved without some space research.

The disadvantage is, of course, money. It's expensive, and you get a lot of people complaining that the money could be used for better purposes. I agree with this argument somewhat but I think the problem is that we need to research things in space or we may face a disaster like an incoming asteroid that we can do nothing about one day.

Q: What are the advantages and disadvantages of watching a sports game on TV compared to watching it live?

A: I think watching a game on TV has several strengths. For example, you can hear the commentary and you can see the action the action repeated again. You are given more knowledge about the game and things are not so noisy for you. You also have the freedom to eat what you want for free and get up and do something else. The seats are more comfortable, and the volume is yours to control. But there is one main disadvantage that is hard to deny. You can't capture the feeling and excitement of watching something live. Also you can't share your joy with other fans at the time that it's happening.

Q: What are the advantages and disadvantages of having a part-time job while at school overseas?

A: I think the main advantage of having a part time job is that it eases the financial burden which is often borne by your parents. You are able to have a little pocket money without going to your parents all the time. Another advantage is that you can generally improve your English a lot if you can work part time overseas. You're working with your colleagues and they can communicate with you daily. The main disadvantage is that it's tiring and the time you spend working could be spent getting good grades. Also, overseas part time work is usually not very well paid so the added pocket money may not really be worth it.

Q: What are the advantages and disadvantages of public transport?

A: I think the main advantage of using public transport is that it's cheap and generally much better for the environment, because you are only using one vehicle instead of many. Especially if your buses run on clean air, you can reduce a lot of emissions. Another advantage of public transport is that it reduces traffic jams. I think public transport is less stressful because you don't have to worry about parking and all that kind of things. The big disadvantage of public transport is the wait. It's much more convenient to just jump in your car and take off. Also, you can to follow a route and you have no flexibility with public transport. Sometimes it can be very uncomfortable, especially during rush hours.

Q: What are the advantages of getting your news from the newspaper?

A: Well, I like knowing what's going on, so newspapers are a good way for me to know what's happening. I won't say that I completely believe everything that I read in the newspapers, but I do find them very interesting and entertaining. I'm sort of an information junkie, so I just like to know current things. Because before a newspaper is printed, the editor will check through the articles and the sources where the news was derived from, it's often more reliable. In TV news, the news broadcaster may say something he or she thinks is right. So I feel newspapers are more reliable.

Q: What are the good things and bad things about Western food?

A: I'm afraid I rarely eat Western food, I'll just make a few guesses then. Let me see... Well, perhaps the good thing about it is that there might not be as much oil since a lot of the food is baked and boiled. I think another good thing is that the hamburgers are quite delicious sometimes. Well, the bad things are many, I think the food is tasteless, at least a lot of the food I've tried. Also, I think hamburgers are quite bad for you and the fat content is very high. That's about all I really know about Western food.

Q: What are the advantages and disadvantages of giving projects in school instead of exams?

A: You know, probably every teacher has weighed the advantages and disadvantages of them. I think the main advantage is that they encourage students to do their own thinking and in the process they take pride in what they create. They also gain more practical knowledge. The problems are mainly related to time. It takes a lot of time, not only for a student to do such a project but also to grade it. Also, how do you grade something like that? To grade something it's hard to be objective.

Q: What are the advantages and disadvantages of a traditional family?

A: Well, my family is quite traditional so I guess I can tell you a bit about this. It's difficult to say what the advantages of a traditional family are. I guess the main thing is that things are probably more stable and everyone knows their role. In my family, for example, we don't really question my father's authority. It's also cheaper for us, because you do everything together as a family. The disadvantage is that you have less freedom to do the things you really want. I mean, it seems that my parents are always questioning my decisions.

Q: What are the advantages and disadvantages of reading books for entertainment compared with watching TV or films?

A: Well, I think the main advantage of reading books is that they do a lot for your imagination. It is more challenging and you have to work harder to gain your knowledge. TV is less challenging and doesn't make you think as much. But the main disadvantage is that books just take too much time to get through. TV is more convenient and time efficient and that's why I think so many people like it.

Q: What are the advantages and disadvantages of living in a small city?

A: Well, I guess the main advantage of living in a small city is that you feel closer to the people around you and so you get a good social life. You have more chances to enjoy nature and the air is much fresher. The disadvantages are the lack of career opportunities and the facilities are generally not as good. Life in a small city may have fresher air and vegetables but it's hard to think about all that when you are worried about sending your kids to a good school.

第三节　问题解决题

1）真题样题：

What do you think we should do to protect the environment?

How do you think global warming can be prevented?

What should one do to prepare for a good trip to China?

从以上例题中可以发现，在口语考试第三类的问题中有一种考题会要求考生针对某一社会现象提出问题并给出合理的解决方法的题型。

2）答题结构：

在这类题型中考生可以按照以下这个步骤来回答：

● Identify the problems

● Suggest solutions

● Suggest definite actions that should be taken

3）答案范例解析：

Interviewer：How would you suggest that the government improve the transport system in your city?

Identify the problems

Student：The transport system is rife with problems：there are too many cars on the roads，there are not enough bus lanes and the subway system is not extensive enough.

Suggest solutions

Student：There are a few measures that can be taken to improve the transport system.

Suggest definite actions that should be taken

Student：The most important thing is to build more roads and be very careful where those roads are built. Then，when there are more and better roads，they can make more bus lanes and extend the subway lines. These are big projects and may take some time，but are necessary if transport problems are to be solved.

4）问题解决题高分细节：

（1）明确地提出问题，如：The system is rife with problems

（2）正确运用提出建议的表达方式，如：they should make an effort to . . .

（3）描述具体的解决方案，如：They should prohibit people from. . .

下面将针对以上高分细节来进行说明

高分细节一:明确地提出问题

首先来看两个例子:

Student:Well,firstly,I think the main problem is that ...

Student:The transport system is rife with problems:there are too many cars on the roads,there are not enough bus lanes and the subway is not extensive enough ...

从以上两个例子中发现,在回答该类问题的开头考生通常首先需要提出对某一社会现象的问题,接下来列举一些在英文中常用的提出问题的方式:

◉There're a lot of problems with ...

例句:There're a lot of problems with the national football team.

◉One major concern with ... that needs addressing is ...

例句:One major concern with the aging population that needs addressing is how we are going to pay for all of those pensions.

◉The biggest problem with ... is ...

例句:The biggest problem with professional sports is that teams become businesses rather than playing for the love of sport.

◉It's unethical to verb ... The main issue many people have with ... is ...

例句:The main issue many people have with warfare is that they feel it is immoral.

高分细节二:正确运用提出建议的表达方式

首先来看两个例子:

Student:... I believe that teachers should be made to go on more-up-date,modern training courses. Secondly,I think that the restaurants... could pay more attention to hygiene and ...

Student:... When there are more and better roads,they can make more bus lanes and extend the subway lines ...

从以上两个例子中可以发现,在讨论问题的过程中考生会针对所提出的问题发表合理的解决方案。接下来,解析一下如何提出解决方案的表达方式:

◉... could do is to make an effort to provide ...

例句:One thing that they could do is to make an effort to provide farmers with more access to better medical care.

◉... should take steps towards dealing with ...

例句：I believe we should take steps towards dealing with the problem of water pollution.

◉... ought to pay more attention to ...

例句：I think that young people ought to pay more attention to how they behave towards old people in public.

◉... should try harder to ...

例句：I am sure that we should try harder to solve the current traffic problems.

◉... could spend more money on ...

例句：The British government could spend more money on public transport，to reduce the cost of travel.

高分细节三：描述具体的解决方案

首先来看两个例子：

Student：... I believe that teachers should be made to go on more-up-date，modern training courses. Secondly，I think that the restaurants ... could pay more attention to hygiene and ...

Student：... another measure would be to encourage people to only buy products from companies that respect the environment ...

从以上两个例子中可以发现，在回答该类问题时，考生在提出建议或者解决方案后需要对解决方案做出具体的描述，使回答更加的具体和完善。接下来列举一些地道的描述解决方案的表达方式和句型：

表达方式：

◉to abolish
◉to spend money on
◉to impose tighter regulations on
◉to put pressure on
◉to encourage people to
◉to renovate

搭配句型：

◉should ＋ verb／phrase

例句：

▶ I strongly believe the authorities should put pressure on factory owners.

▶ I think they should impose tighter regulations on the DVD sales.

▶ I really believe they ought to spend more money on improving the school facilities.

▶ I am convinced that they should abolish certain out-dated laws in this country.

◉by ＋ verb-ing

例句：

▶ They could improve the situation by imposing tighter regulations on . . .

▶ The could improve things by putting pressure on local governments to . . .

▶ We could take measures to solve this problem by spending more money on education.

▶ We can make it a lot better by repairing the damage and by renovating the building . . .

5）真题范例：

Q：What do you think we should do to protect the environment?

A：I think the main challenge is to create a good staff to enforce the standards we have already set. The key thing about a good, clean environment is that the standards be enforced so that the laws have some teeth to them. I also think that it's necessary to have good technical innovations so that the methods to do such things as water treatment can be developed. I also think it really takes a strong commitment by everyone to make sure that the environment is always the top priority in every new plan that is created.

Q：How do you think global warming can be prevented?

A：As far as I know, global warming is caused by the Greenhouse Effect, which results from too much carbon dioxide in the air. I think the government should take measures to limit the number of private cars and make efforts to develop the public transport system. Besides, we should try to replace fossil fuels with new, cleaner energy resources. Once we can reduce the amount of carbon dioxide in the air, the temperatures will very likely stabilize and we can then feel safer that the situation is under control.

Q：What should one do to prepare for a good trip to China?

A：I think you should get a good phrase book that you can use if you need to get things done. You need a basic level of expressions that will help you make your trip easier. You should try to understand the history of China because that will make some of the places that you're going to more interesting. For example, if you watch a film or read a good book on the Forbidden City，it will be much more interesting to you when you wander around in it.

Q：How can traffic be best solved?

A：In my opinions the best way to solve this problem is by trying to widen our roads and build more flyovers at the exits. Shanghai has successfully done this and now experiences fewer problems as a result. I also think that we may have to encourage people to take public transport lines more often or simply ride their bicycles more. One more thing that should be done is to build better smaller roads that connect the bigger roads. One big problem in bigger cities is that a lot of the connecting roads are often blocked and so everyone has to squeeze into some exit roads to get from one area to another.

Q：How can the tourism industry be improved?

A：I believe the first thing to do is to make it illegal for tour operators to collect commissions from various shops or stores and to simply increase the salaries of the tour operators. The second thing that needs to be done is there needs to be more control over the vendors in the famous sites to make sure they don't harass visitors. It can be very unpleasant when people follow you everywhere to sell their things. Finally，I think that there should be more opportunities to do independent travelling by setting up more campsites and clean hostels，to accept the backpacking crowds.

Q：How can education be reformed to meet future challenges?

A：I guess the best reforms should be in the area of post secondary education and I think it would be good to pour a lot of money into upgrading the facilities and attracting better university professors to work in them. I also think there should be more community colleges and smaller universities that accept people from all walks of life. One more thing is that I think there should be more opportunities for distance learning programs from various universities around the world so that many Chinese can get benefit from overseas education without travelling so far to other countries.

Q：How can we preserve our history best?

A：I believe the best way to preserve our history is to make sure that we protect the symbols of our history，and that means that we try to set aside enough room for our old buildings and old sections of town to flourish. I think it's important to make sure that we also try to provide some reenactments of history in our films，books and TV shows and also，if possible，through our tourist areas. I think another very important way is by keeping good records of the events that take place and by getting a variety of interpretations of history.

第七章　雅思口语实例纠错

中国考生的口语存在着一些普遍问题,如发音、口音、流利度欠缺等,但是其实最为严重的是,很多考生自创中式表达,也就是我们所熟知的中式英语(Chinglish)。其实很多人已经对一些非常 popular 的中式英语耳熟能详,比如说 people mountain people sea 等,但是还是有很多错误的英语句子是中国学生没有意识到,而且经常使用的。现归纳如下:

1) I very much like David Beckham.

其实这种说法还是比较普遍的。very 虽说是个副词,但是并不能像一般的副词一样,放在副词前面修饰动词,所以 very 有自己独特的用法。这句话正确的写法是:I like David Beckham very much. 但是老外更习惯于说 I am a huge fan of David Beckham;I am insanely crazy about him;I could think of nobody that tops him;其次,在口语表达中,很多学生习惯于用 very good 这种表达方式。这里向各位考生推荐其他的一些表达方式,如 incredible,amazing,unbelievable,impressive,awesome 等。

2) My English is poor.

很多考生看到这句话,第一反应就是:"这句话还是错的吗?我们老师就是这么教我们的!"其实,在英语表达里面,尤其是口语,单纯的语法正确并不能表明这句话的意思就是对的。我从来没有听过老外讲过 My Chinese is poor. 口语中更加注重的是语言表达习惯。虽然某句话是对的,但是没有人这么讲。老外通常会讲 My Chinese sucks;My Chinese is awful. 更多的情况下,老外的表达会比较积极,比如说 I am getting better though ...

3) Oral English

曾经听到很多的学生说 oral English,甚至还包括个别的外教。根据我对这个词的了解,oral English 并不能表示 spoken English。后来,我问了很多外教,确认了我的判断是正确的。在英文里面,oral 更多的是表示跟口腔有关的意思。口语更多的是用 spoken English 或者 speaking English 来表示。外教们在中国时间待长了,也会被同化,犯这种错误,但是他们回到自己的国家后就会立刻改过来。但是对于我们中国数千万的莘莘学子来讲,在中国这个大环境下,这样的错误如果不及时纠正的话,恐怕就是一辈子都会犯的错误了。

4) Cliché

还有一些中国考生经常存在的问题,从严格意义上来讲,并不是一些错误,只是说被中国考生用烂掉了,所以雅思考官听到就会反感了。比如说:

• a lot of

这个词组并没有什么错误,只是当所有学生都在用的时候,它就自然而然变成了"错误"的。我们可以用很多替代的词,例如:There are tons of people in the classroom; I have been to like a million interviews 等等。

• I think

中国考生很喜欢用一些 stereotyped 答案。比如说考官问你问题的时候,很多考生就习惯于回答 I think ... 其实,从英语角度来讲,I think 代表一种不确定性,所以当你在表达观点加上这么一个词的时候,就是表达一种不确定的概念给考官,所以建议考生们尽量避免这个表达。

• maybe

很多考生用 maybe 来表达 probably(极有可能地)的概念,其实这是大错特错的。maybe,更加确切的意思,表示应该怎么样,但是这种可能性并不大。比如说:

Since you are so incredibly talented, maybe it's time for you to compete for the Emmy Awards.

George W. Bush administration has always been standing in the way of other countries' economic development. Maybe they love to present themselves as a head-scratching problem to the world.

第八章 雅思口语兵工厂

在这个章节里面,我们收录了包括口语考试常见疑问,口语表达常用句型,常用谚语与俚语等内容,以供大家备考之用。

一、实用句型

1) 表明自己的观点:

In my opinion, . . .	In my point of view, . . .
As far as I am concerned, . . .	As for me, . . .
From where I stand . . .	I'd like to point out that . . .
It seems to me that . . .	What I reckon is . . .
Frankly speaking, . . .	To be honest, . . .
Actually, . . .	Personally, . . .
To tell the truth . . .	I agree with . . .
It depends, different people have different . . .	It is difficult for me to make a choice (tell the differences), you know . . . (on one hand . . . on the other hand . . .)
Well, it is an interesting / tough question, because . . .	I am not much of a . . . , so I know little about . . . but I guess . . .

2) 表示原因

Because(of) . . .	Since . . .
As . . .	Due to . . . , . . .
We attribute . . . to . . .	We owe . . . to . . .
Thanks to . . .	Now that . . .
On account of . . .	. . . leads to . . .
. . . is responsible for . . .	. . . results in . . .

3）举例说明

Let me give you an example.	To make it clear to you, . . .
Take . . . for instance . . .	

4）表示对某事物感兴趣

I'm fairly keen on . . .	I'm really into . . .
I'm a big fan of . . .	I simply adore . . .
I'm quite enthusiastic / passionate about . . .	I generally prefer . . . to . . .
I'm pretty fond of . . .	I'm totally mad about . . .
I'm obsessed with . . .	I'm fascinated by . . .
. . . is my cup of tea.	I can't find words to express how much I like . . .

5）表示自己的观点与别人不同

Some people may regard . . . as . . . , however，I just don't buy it.	I can find my agreement in this argument . . . , In my opinion，. . .
Some think . . . while I . . .	I don't agree with those people who hold a firm view that . . .

6）用另一种方式重述

In other words，. . .	What I'm trying to say is . . .
Perhaps I should make that clearer by saying . . .	Let me put it another way . . .
If I can rephrase that . . .	The point I'm making is that . . .
It's probably more accurate to say . . .	

7）简单却可以画龙点睛的连接词

Well	Actually
In fact	You see
You know	How shall I put it
Let me think for a second	

二、实用谚语

1) A bosom friend afar brings a distant land near. 海内存知己, 天涯若比邻。

2) A common danger causes common action. 同舟共济。

3) A contented mind is a continual / perpetual feast. 知足常乐。

4) A fall into the pit, a gain in your wit. 吃一堑, 长一智。

5) A guest should suit the convenience of the host. 客随主便。

6) A letter from home is a priceless treasure. 家书抵万金。

7) All rivers run into the sea. 殊途同归。

8) All time is no time when it is past. 机不可失, 时不再来。

9) An apple a day keeps the doctor away. 一日一个苹果, 身体健康不求医。

10) As heroes think, so thought Bruce. 英雄所见略同。

11) A young idler, an old beggar. 少壮不努力, 老大徒伤悲。

12) Behind the mountains there are people to be found. 天外有天, 山外有山。

13) Bad luck often brings good luck. 塞翁失马, 焉知非福。

14) Bread is the stall of life. 面包是生命的支柱。(民以食为天。)

15) Business is business. 公事公办。

16) Clumsy birds have to start flying early. 笨鸟先飞。

17) Courtesy costs nothing. 礼多人不怪。

18) Custom makes all things easy. 习惯成自然。

19) Desire has no rest. 人的欲望无止境。

20) Difficult the first time, easy the second. 一回生, 二回熟。

21) Do not change horses in mid-stream. 别在河流中间换马。

22) Do not have too many irons in the fire. 贪多嚼不烂。

23) Do not pull all your eggs in one basket. 别把所有的蛋都放在一个篮子里。(不要孤注一掷。)

24) Do not teach fish to swim. 不要班门弄斧。

25) East or west, home is the best. 东奔西跑, 还是家里好。(金窝银窝, 不如自己的狗窝)。

26) Experience is the best teacher. 实践出真知。

27) Fact is stranger than fiction. 事实比虚构更离奇。(大千世界, 无奇不有。)

28) Faith can move mountains. 信念能移山。(精诚所至, 金石为开。)

29) First impressions are half the battle. 先入为主。

30) Give as good as one gets. 一报还一报。(以德报德, 以怨还怨。)

31) Give everyone his due. 一视同仁。

32) Good wine needs no bush. 酒香不怕巷子深。

33) Haste makes waste. 欲速则不达。(忙中常出错。)

34) He that promises too much means nothing. 轻诺者寡信。

35) He who has an art has everywhere a part. 一招鲜,吃遍天。

36) He would climb the ladder must begin at the bottom. 千里之行始于足下。

37) Home is where the heart is. 心在哪里,哪里就是家。

38) If you are not inside a house, you do not know about its leaking. 不在屋里,不知漏雨。(亲身经历才有体会。)

39) In peace prepare for war. 平时准备战时。(居安思危。)

40) It is never too late to mend. 亡羊补牢,犹未为晚。

41) It six of one and half a dozen of the other. 彼此彼此。

42) Just has long arms. 法网恢恢,疏而不漏。

43) Keep something for a rainy day. 未雨绸缪。

44) Life is a span. 人生如朝露。

45) Man proposes, God disposes. 谋事在人,成事在天。

46) Meet plot with plot. 将计就计。

47) Merry meet, merry part. 好聚好散。

48) Mind acts upon mind. 心有灵犀一点通。

49) Never hit a man when he is down. 不要落井下石。

50) Never judge by appearances. 切莫以貌取人。

51) No fire without smoke. 无风不起浪。

52) Nurture passes nature. 教养胜过天性。

53) One is never too old to learn. 活到老,学到老。

54) One swallow does not make a summer. 一燕不成夏。(一枝独放不是春。)

55) One who has seen the ocean thinks nothing of mere rivers. 曾经沧海难为水。

56) Out of sight, out of mind. 眼不见,心不烦。

57) Practice makes perfect. 熟能生巧。

58) Poverty is stranger to industry. 勤劳之人不受穷。

59) Rome was not built in a day. 罗马不是一日建成的。(伟业非一日之功。)

60) Sense comes with age. 老马识途。

61) So many men, so many minds. 人心各不同。

62) Some thing is learned every time a book is opened. 开卷有益。

63) Strike while the iron is hot. 趁热打铁。

64) The car will find its way round the hill when it gets there. 车到山前必有路。

65) The heart is seen in wine. 酒后吐真言。

66) The older,the wiser. 人老智多。(姜还是老的辣。)

67) The worse luck now, the better another time. 风水轮流转。

68) Thoughts are free from toll. 思想不用交税。(人人都可以自由思考。)

69) Time tries all things. 时间检验一切。

70) Use legs and have legs. 经常用腿,健步如飞。

71）Virtue never grows old. 美德常青。

72）Walls have ears. 隔墙有耳。

73）What is done cannot be undone. 覆水难收。

74）Wine in，truth out. 酒后吐真言。

75）You are only young once. 青春只有一次。

76）You cannot burn the candle at both ends. 蜡烛不可两头燃。（鱼和熊掌不可兼得。）

77）You cannot have your cake and eat it. 有得就有失。（事难两全其美。）

78）You never know till you have tried. 事非经过不知难。

79）Youth will be served. 青春好作乐。

80）Zeal without knowledge is a runaway horse. 无知的狂热是脱缰的野马。

三、实用俚语

1）Be in the air 将要发生的事情

The feeling or idea that something new is about to happen or is going to change.

Example：From the arguments going on at the meeting，it seems that a change in policy is in the air.

2）Clear the air 消除误会

To settle a dispute and restore good relations

Example：We had a meeting with the workers，and I think we've cleared the air now.

3）Cost an arm and a leg 极其昂贵的

To be very expensive

Example：I love that fur coat. However，I don't think I'm going to buy it because it costs an arm and a leg.

4）A bad egg 缺乏道德的人

Somebody who has no moral principles and should be avoided

Example：You mustn't lend Tim money，he's a bad egg. You'll never see him or your money again!

5）In the bag 稳操胜券

Said of an achievement which is secure

Example：We have the deal in the bag. The client came in this morning to sign the agreement.

6）In the balance 未知的，不可预测的

Said when the outcome of a situation is unknown or unpredictable

Example：His career as a pilot is in the balance，as his eyesight does not seem good enough.

7）Drive a hard bargain 极力讨价还价

To have the negotiating strength and skills to get the most advantageous price and conditions

Example：Amanda is negotiating the best price from the suppliers. She drives a hard bargain.

8）Ring a bell 看上去或听起来非常熟悉

To look，sound or seem familiar

Example：That face rings a bell，where have I seen him before?

9）Tighten one's belt 节衣缩食

To cut down on spending because there is less income than before

Example：Now you are out of work，you'll have to tighten your belt and give up buying new clothes and going out so often.

10）Kill two birds with one stone 一石二鸟

To complete two tasks together，with less effort than doing them separately

Example：Since I'd gone to the store to buy some bread，I thought of killing two birds with one stone and invited Mr. Biggs to the party.

11）Be in a black mood 情绪极差

To be so negative about everything that it is impossible for anyone to reason with him / her

Example：My father has been in a black mood for days，we dare not say anything to him.

12）New blood 新成员

New people brought into an organization to introduce different and original ideas

Example：It was decided to bring new blood into the school by employing teachers with the latest training.

13）Feeling blue 感到无精打采

Feeling sad or depressed

Example：She's feeling blue，because the man she loves is far away.

14）Get to the bottom of something 弄清真相

To find out the truth about something

Example：I'm trying to get to the bottom of why David left without saying goodbye.

15）A piece of cake 轻松的事

Something which is very easy to do

Example：Here . . . let me put the batteries in for you. It's a piece of cake.

16）Pay a call 拜访

To visit somebody

Example：As we're in this neighborhood，we might as well pay the Jacksons a call，we haven't seen them for ages.

17）By chance 偶然，意外的

Unexpectedly；with no prior planning

Example：By chance, I bumped into my wife in the shopping mall.

18）Round the clock 夜以继日的

To do something continuously, without a break or pause

Example：The ambulance services worked round the clock hauling people trapped in the building to safety.

19）Keep one's cool 保持冷静

To stay calm in a difficult situation

Example：If the traffic is jamed, the only thing to do is keep your cool, or get out of the car and walk！

20）In a tight corner 处于困境

In an extremely difficult situation

Example：Whenever I get into a tight corner, I try to rely on quick thinking to get out of it.

四、实用词汇

1）人物

easygoing 随和的	compassionate 有同情心的	good-natured 性格好的
bad-tempered 性格不好的	optimistic 乐观的	pessimistic 悲观的
introverted 内向的	extroverted 外向的	person of the year 风云人物
world-renown 世界闻名	prestigious 声明远播的	notorious 臭名昭著的
talent 才华	trend-setting 带动潮流的	contribution 贡献
high media exposure 媒体曝光率	selflessness 无私	adventurous 勇于尝试的
responsible and stand by me 在我身边给我鼓励和支持	enforce curfew 宵禁（必须回家的时间）	conscientious 认真负责
value 价值观	moral 道德观	impact 对生活的影响
world perspective 世界观	lack of understanding 不理解	loving and caring 有爱心的
generation gap 代沟	no privacy 没有隐私	bossy 好管事的
disciplinarian 纪律严明	You're grounded. 不许出门。	patient 耐心
My way or the highway. 要么听我的，要么滚出去。	close-knit family 家庭关系紧密，观念强，常联系的家庭	dysfunctional family 家庭功能不健全，问题多多家庭

extended family 大家	bi-racial family 国际家庭	nuclear family 小家
breadwinner 养家的人	hands-off 放手	trusting 信任孩子
reserved 有所保留的	role model 行为榜样,模范	good communicator 善于沟通的人

2）食物

cabbage 卷心菜	cucumber 黄瓜	Chinese cabbage 白菜
spinach 菠菜	Chinese squash 南瓜	mushroom 蘑菇
carrot 胡萝卜	ginger 姜	tomato 番茄
potato 马铃薯	sweet potato 红薯	eggplant 茄子
garlic 蒜	onion 洋葱	chili 辣椒
strawberry 草莓	date 枣	mandarin orange 橘子
watermelon 西瓜	lemon 柠檬	coconut 椰子
peach 桃	plum 李子,梅子	litchi 荔枝
pineapple 菠萝	kiwi 猕猴桃	grapefruit 葡萄柚
apricot 杏	cherry 樱桃	mango 芒果
pomegranate 石榴	olive 橄榄	grape 葡萄
raspberry 木莓	blackberry 黑莓	fig 无花果
yogurt 酸牛奶	soda water 汽水	herb juice 青草茶
black tea 红茶	green tea 绿茶	instant coffee 速溶咖啡
milkshake 奶昔	mineral water 矿泉水	lemonade 柠檬汁
champagne 香槟	wine 葡萄酒	appetiser 开胃菜
soybean milk 豆浆	boiled dumplings 水饺	steamed dumplings 蒸饺
sweet dumpling, rice glue ball 元宵	steamed buns 馒头	eggs cakes 蛋饼
rice porridge 稀饭,粥	fried rice with egg 蛋炒饭	plain white rice 白米饭
restaurant 饭店,餐馆	take-away food restaurant 外卖店	take-out 食品外卖
fast food restaurant 快餐店	canteen 食堂	pub 酒馆
dining-hall 餐厅	snack bar 小吃部	cafeteria 自助餐厅
feast 盛宴	unique flavor 风味独特	sanitation 卫生

3）娱乐

traditional music 传统音乐	classical music 古典音乐	light music 轻音乐
dancing music 舞曲	pop music 流行音乐	folk music 民间音乐
country music 乡村音乐	Jazz（music）爵士乐	rock-and-roll 摇滚乐
blues 布鲁斯，蓝调	swing 摇摆乐	folk songs 民歌
campus songs 校园歌曲	art ballad 艺术民谣或歌曲	world famous piece of music 世界名曲
civic ballad 民谣	national music 民族音乐	art songs 艺术歌曲
energetic 充满活力的	soulful 充满热情的	interesting or pleasant to listen to 动听的
soothing 抚慰的，使人宽心的	sentimental 感伤的	inspiring 鼓舞的
strong beat 强烈的节奏	feel void 感到空虚	tuneful 和谐的，音调谐美的
nostalgic 怀旧的	encouraging 激励人的	ease pressure 减压
romantic 浪漫的	escape 逃避，解脱	kill time 消磨时间
easy to understand 容易理解	refresh one's mind 使人清醒	melodious, rising and falling 悠扬的
distraction 娱乐，分心，分心的事物	pleasant 悦耳的	melody 悦耳的音调
personal preference 个人喜好	pastime, recreation 消遣，娱乐	tedious 单调乏味的，沉闷的，冗长乏味的
memorable 难忘的	thrilling 刺激的	nostalgic 怀旧的
artistic 艺术的，有美感的	ravishing 引人入胜的	heyday 全盛期
hit 卖座影片	box-office 票房	footage 影片长度
on-screen 银幕上的	profitable 有利可图的	title 片名
original version 原著	dialogue 对白	subtitle, subtitling 字幕
film industry 电影工业	screenplay 电影剧本	action star 动作明星
motion-picture 动作片	independent films 独立影片	feature films 故事片
documentary 纪录片	epic film 史诗片	Kung fu film 武打片
romantic movie 爱情片	newsreel 新闻片	literary film 文艺片
musical 音乐片	comedy 喜剧片	tragedy 悲剧片
Dracula movie 恐怖片	swordsmen film 武侠片	detective film 侦探片
ethical film 伦理片	western movie 西部片	film advant-garde 前卫片
serial 系列片	trailer 预告片	cartoon（film）动画片

4) 新闻媒体

Internet 网络	magazine 杂志	newspaper 报纸
quarterly 季刊	radio 广播	TV 电视
weekly 周报	daily 日报	monthly 月刊
scoop "抢"（新闻）	makeup 版面设计	scandal 丑闻
reader's interest 读者兴趣	quality paper 高级报纸，严肃报纸	fast update 更新（新闻内容）快
sidebar 花絮新闻	readability 可读性	tip 内幕新闻，秘密消息
hot news 热点新闻	human interest 人情味	profile 人物专访，人物特写
trim 删改（稿件）	in-depth reporting 深度报道	timeliness 时效性，时新性
sensational 耸人听闻的，具有轰动效应的	sex scandal 桃色新闻	hearsay 小道消息
news value 新闻价值	suspended interest 悬念	highlight 要闻
blank "开天窗"	suspended 更新（新闻内容），增强（时效性）	clipping 剪报
brief 简讯	objectivity 客观性	continued story 连载故事，连载小说
pseudo event 假新闻	press 报界，新闻界	chart 每周流行音乐排行版
opinion poll 民意测验	periodical 期刊	mass media 大众传播媒介
libel 诽谤（罪）	cover girl 封面女郎	exclusive 独家新闻
anecdote 趣闻轶事	profile 人物专访，人物特写	correspondence column 读者来信专栏
editorial 社论	remuneration 稿费	banner 通栏标题
news agency 通讯社	digest 文摘	extra 号外
subhead 小标题，副标题	bulletin 新闻简报	news clue 新闻线索
covert coverage 隐性采访，秘密采访	press conference 新闻发布会，记者招待台	press release 新闻公告，新闻简报
free-lancer 自由撰稿人	columnist 专栏作家	back alley news 小道消息

5) 旅游

honeymoon trip 蜜月旅行	independent / do-it-yourself travel 自助游	wedding vacation 婚假
group travel 随团旅游	wedding travel 旅行结婚	luxury tour (travel) 豪华标准游

outbound tourism 出境游	package trip，package tour 包办旅游	inbound tourism 国内游
summer resort 避暑地	to be laid out appropriately 布局得宜	resplendent，brilliant 璀璨的
to tour abroad 出国旅游	to sightsee，to go sightseeing 观光	scenic spots 风景点
picturesque landscape 风景如画	historic site，site of historic importance 古迹	winter scenery 冬景
famous mountains and great rivers 名山大川	place of interest，interesting scenic spot 名胜	sand scenery 沙漠风光
landscape scenery 山水风光	natural cave 天然洞穴	cultural heritage 文化遗产
cultural legacy 文化遗产	cultural relics 文物	coastal city 沿海城市

6）科技

deterioration 变坏,退化,堕落	creativity 创造力,创造	virus 病毒
endangered species 濒危物种	catastrophe 大灾难,大祸	computer virus 电脑病毒
creativity 创造力,创造	software 软件	online chat 上网聊天
e-commerce 电子商务	upgrade 升级	alienate 疏远
industrial pollutant 工业污染物	recycling 废物再利用	water pollution 水污染
depletion 损耗	breakthrough 突破	Netsurfing 网络冲浪
environment deterioration 环境恶化	exhausted gas 尾气	jeopardize 危害
download 下载	offload 卸载	hardware 硬件
clone 克隆	air polluter 空气污染源	noise pollution 噪音污染
energy shortage 能源短缺	fatal 致命的,重大的	destructive power 破坏力
automatic 自动化的	millennium bug 千年虫	advancement 前进,进步

7）教育

educational background 教育程度	educational history 学历	curriculum 课程
major 主修	minor 副修	educational highlights 课程重点部分
curriculum included 课程包括	specialized courses 专门课程	courses taken 所学课程

courses completed 完成课程	special training 特别训练	social practice 社会实践
part-time jobs 业余工作	summer jobs 暑期工作	vacation jobs 假期工作
refresher course 进修课程	extracurricular activities 课外活动	physical activities 体育活动
recreational activities 娱乐活动	academic activities 学术活动	social activities 社会活动
rewards 奖励	scholarship 奖学金	excellent League member 优秀团员
excellent leader 优秀干部	student council 学生会	off-job training 脱产培训
in-job training 在职培训	educational system 学制	academic year 学年
semester 学期（美）	term 学期（英）	president 校长
vice-president 副校长	dean 院长	assistant dean 副院长
academic dean 教务长	department chairman 系主任	professor 教授
associate professor 副教授	guest professor 客座教授	lecturer 讲师
teaching assistant 助教	research fellow 研究员	research assistant 助理研究员
supervisor 论文导师	principal 中学校长（美）	headmaster 中学校长（英）
master 小学校长（美）	dean of studies 教务长	dean of students 教导主任
probation teacher 代课教师	tutor 家庭教师	intelligence quotient 智商
pass 及格	fail 不及格	marks 分数
grades 分数	scores 分数	

8) 家乡

modern 现代	hospitable and friendly 好客且友善的	cosmopolitan 四海一家的国际化大都市
passionate, enthusiastic 激情，热情	metropolitan 大都市	tourist attractions and historical interests 旅游景点，历史古籍
urban / suburban / rural area 城区/郊区/农村	souvenirs 纪念品	shopping malls 购物中心
transportation 交通	urban conveniences 市区的便利	industrial pattern 工业布局
rush hour 交通高峰期	city-dweller 城市居民	necessary facilities 必要设施
city planning 城市规划	well-fed 吃得好	heavy purchase 大采购

well-informed 受过教育的	well-developed 发达的	culturally diverse 文化多元化的
chaos，confusion 混乱	infrastructure 基础设施	serious pollution 污染严重
soaring crime rate 急剧上升的犯罪率	adequate supply of goods 物品供应充足	transportation 交通
recreation 消遣	convenient traffic 交通方便	night life 夜生活
traffic jam 交通阻塞	first-rate healthcare 一流的医疗保健	employment opportunity 就业机会
well-dressed 衣着光鲜的	air pollution 空气污染	exotic culture 异国文化
cross-cultural communication 跨文化交际	concert hall 音乐厅	trendy 流行的
overcrowding 拥挤的	gallery 美术馆	crowded 拥挤
promising future 前景光明	prestigious university 有名的大学	lack of security 缺乏安全
entertainment 娱乐	easy assess to news 容易获得消息	recreational facilities 娱乐设施
cost of living 生活费用	exhibition 展览	quietness 安静
backward 落后的	longevity 长寿	tranquil / quiet living 生活宁静
tedious 沉闷的，乏味的	idyllic 田园诗般的	monotonous 单调的
uninformed 消息闭塞的	low crime rate 低犯罪率	fresh air 新鲜的空气
harmonious 和谐的	safety，security 安全	clean environment 环境清洁
inconvenience 麻烦，不方便之处	simple 简单的	spacious 宽敞的
cheap living expenses 低生活成本	free from a contaminated environment 远离受污染的环境	villa 别墅
hall 殿	balconied house 带阳台的房屋	reinforced concrete building 钢筋混凝土建筑
high-rise building 高层建筑	apartment 公寓	beach villa 海滨别墅
dormitory 集体宿舍	hut 简陋小屋	old-fashioned house 老式房屋
two-storied house 两层楼房	low-rise 两层以下无电梯建筑物	skyscraper 摩天大楼
wooden architecture 木结构建筑	slum 贫民窟	courtyard dwellings 四合院

| temple 寺,庙 | landscape architecture 园林建筑 | brick building 砖结构建筑 |
| religious architecture 宗教建筑 | corridor 走廊 | |

9）工作

routine 例行的；常规的	career 事业	profession 职业
individual success 个人成功	work overtime 加班	laid off 下岗
contribute to / make contribute to 贡献	balance between 平衡	preoccupied with 忙于
be replaced 被淘汰	benefits 福利	head hunter 猎头
human resource 人力资源	meaning in life 生命的意义	promotions 升职
under stress 承受压力	job hopping 跳槽	intense competition 激烈竞争
self-worth 自我价值	being in a team 在团队中	learn from your boss 跟老板学习
contribute to social progress and stability 为社会进步和稳定作贡献	become an able, worthy and useful person 成为有能力、有价值、有用之人	become fast friend with your colleagues 和同事交朋友
receptionist 接待员,传达员	typist 打字员	programmer 程序师,程序规划员
office girl 女记事员	public servant 公务员	pilot 飞行员
publisher 出版者,发行人	graphic designer 美术设计	secretary 秘书,书记
policeman 警察	journalist 记者	editor 编辑,编者
interpreter 口译员,讲解员	director 主任,主管,导演	photographer 摄影师
scholar 学者	translator 翻译者	novelist(长篇)小说家
playwright 剧作家	linguist 语言学家	botanist 植物学家
economist 经济学家	chemist 化学家,药剂师	scientist 科学家
philosopher 哲学家,哲人	politician 政治家,政客	physicist 物理学者
archaeologist 考古学家	geologist 地质学者	mathematician 数学家
biologist 生物学家	zoologist 动物学家	physiologist 生理学者
artist 艺术家,画家	painter 画家	musician 音乐家
composer 作曲家,设计者	singer 歌手	designer 设计家,制图师
dressmaker 裁缝	beautician 美容师	model 模特儿

clerk 职员,办事员	copywriter 广告文编写人	producer （电影）制片人
pharmacist 配药者,药剂师	architect 建筑师	tour guide 导游
civil planner 城市设计师	civil engineer 土木技师	dentist 牙科医生

10) 法律

criminal 罪犯	victim 受害者	witness 目击证人
witness box 证人席	arrest 拘捕	courtroom 法庭
judge 法官	bench （法官坐的）审判台	jury 陪审团
jury box 陪审席	defendant 被告	transcript 纪录;副本
prosecution attorney 主控律师	defence attorney 辩方律师	fingerprints 手指模
penalty 罚款,惩罚	tough penalties 很高的罚款	punishment 惩罚
sentence 宣判	prison 监狱、囚禁	drug trafficker 贩毒的人
uneducated 文盲的	replica 复制品	qualified 有资格的
weapon 武器,兵器	imprisonment 入狱	convict 宣判有罪
illegal 非法的,犯法的	handcuff 手铐	baton 警棍
walkie-talkie 对讲机	behaviour 品行	fine punishment 罚金
robber 盗贼,强盗	robbery 盗窃（罪）	commits 犯罪
murderer 杀人者	murder 谋杀（罪）	arson 纵火（罪）
burglar 夜贼	burglary 夜盗（罪）	drug trafficking 贩毒
thief 小偷	theft 偷窃（罪）	

11) 环境气候

hail 冰雹	sleet 冰雨	hurricane 飓风
heavy rain 雷雨	thundershower 雷阵雨	tornado 龙卷风
downpour 倾盆大雨	lightning 闪电	frost 霜冻
typhoon 台风	weather 天气	breeze 微风
whirlwind 旋风	smog 烟雾	gusty 阵风
shower 阵雨	moderate rain 中雨	freeze 冰冻
mist 薄雾	humidity 潮湿	spring breeze 春风

humid 潮湿的	moist 潮湿的	pleasantly warm 春风和煦的
spring chill 春寒料峭	strong wind 大风	heavy rain 大雨
foggy 多雾的	heavy snow 大雪	rainy 多雨的
overcast 多云的,阴天	cloudy 多云的	dry 干燥的
high temperature 高温的	plateau climate 高原气候	genial sunshine 和煦的阳光
continental climate 大陆性气候	a clear and crisp autumn day 秋高气爽的日子	extraordinary weather 反常天气
fresh air 空气新鲜.	thunder 雷	below zero 零下
stuffy 闷热的	mild weather 气候温和	snowfall 降雪
hurricane 飓风	severe weather 恶劣的天气	a nice / fine day 天气晴朗
gloomy 天气阴郁的	warm weather 温暖的天气	fog 雾
drizzle 小雨	snowflake 雪花	sunny 阳光灿烂的
agreeable weather 宜人的气候	overcast 阴暗的	pleasant，delightful 宜人的
white pollution 白色污染	urbanization 城市化	fly ash 飞灰
integrated waste management 废物综合治理	on the verge of extinction 处于灭绝的边缘	endangered species 濒危的物种
overexploit 过度开发	biodegradable 可生物降解的	afforestation 绿化造林
industrial dust pollution 工业粉尘污染	break the ecological balance 破坏生态平衡	dumping chemical wastes 倾倒化工废物
deforestation 森林砍伐	desertification 沙漠化	biodiversity 生物多样性
acid rain 酸雨	solar energy 太阳能	landfill 填埋场
soil erosion 土壤腐蚀	vegetation 植被	marsh gas 沼气
noxious fume 有毒气体	poisonous gases 有毒气体	toxic gas 有毒气体
birth rate 出生率	only child 独生子(女)	birth control 节育,避孕
family planning policy 计划生育政策	abortion 流产	needy 贫穷的
poverty 贫困	poverty-line 贫困线	poverty-stricken 贫困的
average life span 人均寿命	population explosion 人口爆炸,人口激增	thickly-populated 人口稠密的
overpopulation 人口过度	population control 人口控制	life expectancy 预期寿命
illiteracy, illiterate 文盲	eligible children 适龄儿童	conservative 守旧的

12) 动物

ox 牛	buffalo 水牛	bull 公牛
calf 小牛，牛犊	cow 母牛	puppy 小狗
ass，donkey 驴	mule 骡	kitten 小猫
horse 马	mare 母马	pony 矮马
goat 山羊	lamb 羊羔，羔羊	sheep 羊
ewe 母羊	pig 猪	piglet 猪崽
white dolphin 白海豚	wild cat 野猫	elephant 大象
wolf 狼	crocodile 鳄鱼	zebra 斑马
leopard 豹	giraffe 长颈鹿	kangaroo 袋鼠
koala 考拉，树袋熊	dromedary 单峰驼	hare 野兔
beaver 河狸	bison 美洲野牛	hippopotamus 河马
dolphin 河豚	duckbill，platypus 鸭嘴兽	monkey 猴子
fox 狐狸	mouse 家鼠	deer 鹿
camel 骆驼	gorilla 大猩猩	bat 蝙蝠
lion 狮	anteater 食蚁兽	antelope 羚羊
rat 鼠	reindeer 驯鹿	rhinoceros 犀牛
otter 水獭	tiger 虎	squirrel 松鼠
walrus 海象	seal 海豹	whale 鲸
marmot 土拨鼠	mole 鼹鼠	hedgehog 刺猬
chimpanzee 黑猩猩	orangutan 猩猩	gorilla 大猩猩

五、口语考试 FAQ

关于口语考试比较笼统的问题：

1) 每个考生的口语话题是一样的吗？

不是。关于问题和话题，每个考生可能会有多种选择，因此没有完全一样的考试。

2) 我可以带什么进考场？

你只需携带个人的身份证件。考官会提供考试中所需的所有用品。

3) 为什么雅思口语需要记录下来？

记录是因为有时考官需要对考生的成绩予以点评。

4）背诵一些关于家乡或工作的简短用语是不是个好方法呢？

这种做法是不可取的。考试中,你应该仔细聆听考官的问题并予以回答。通过死记硬背"标准答案"回答时通常会抓不住问题的重点,本末倒置,并且会影响发音。

5）雅思考试中,口语能像阅读和听力一样计半分吗？

可以。口语成绩以整数值或半分值记录,因此你的成绩可以是 6 或 7 分,以及 6.5 分。

6）考官会对我的考试情况给予任何反馈吗？

不会。考官是不允许做出反馈的,同时你也不能向考官询问你的考试结果。

关于口语考试第一部分的问题：

1）第一部分的考查目的是什么？

考官想考查一下你如何回答一些简单的话题,比如你的学习或工作、日常生活和兴趣爱好等,从而了解你是否能流利地表达关于自己以及日常情况的问题。较之更抽象的话题,个人话题通常更易于表述。

2）考官在第一部分会涉及什么话题？

开始,考官会问一些关于自我介绍的问题。回答时,应该做到简洁明了。考官会提出任何一般性的、日常性的话题,这时你就需要心中有数。正常情况下,考官会围绕三个话题进行提问,并清楚地介绍每一个新话题。因此当你回答一个话题的问题时,应该准备不同的话题。

3）考官会问什么样的问题？

问题很简单。会让你描述自己的喜好、日常生活、计划等等。有时,会让你描述关于过去、现在或将来的话题。有时会让你简单地表述一下自己的意见。

4）回答需要多长时间？

第一部分回答不应太长,但一定要完整。回答应该保持连贯,不要有太多的停顿。同时你的思维要连贯紧密。如果你的回答总是太短的话,考官不会给你高分的。

5）如果没有什么可说时怎么办？

记住一点:第一部分是关于个人信息的。所以你可以引用个人经历,大胆表达自己对某事的想法。

6）怎样提高口语的语法准确性呢？

仔细听问题,从而帮助你判断时态并做出回答。避免使用自己不熟悉的单词。

7）没有理解考官提出的问题时该如何应对？

你可以让考官重复一下问题或者让其用另一种方式表达一下。但是,如果大多数问题你不能理解,在回答之前必须认真听问题。

关于口语考试第二部分的问题:

1) 第二部分的考查目的是什么?

这一部分,考官会让你围绕个人经历就一个简单话题作出简短的回答。旨在考查你自己是否能用英语表述1—2分钟。

2) 考试中需要自己计时吗?

不需要。考官会为考试的各个部分进行计时。关于第二部分,回答时间不会超过两分钟,到时考官会提示停止。但是,你需要知道两分钟是多长,以便你适时地组织语言。

3) 第二部分的形式是怎样的?

考官会提供文本,文本上面有需要你展开表述的话题以及指导你如何回答的要点。

4) 如果不理解话题中的部分单词时该怎么办?

你可以让考官解释你不理解的任何单词。

5) 需要花多长时间做笔记?

考官会给你一分钟的时间做笔记。期间,她/他不会和你讲话。笔记不计入分数,考完之后会被扔掉。笔记不能带离考场。

6) 1分钟的准备时间还没有结束时可以开始作答吗?

可以。如果你不用花1分钟时间,准备好的话就可以开始作答了。但是,充分利用1分钟的时间是明智的。

7) 如果没有某一话题的经历该怎么办?

选出的话题都是人人普遍经历过的,因此你不需要用特殊的语言来表达。考生不会回答给出话题的情况几乎是没有的。但是真的无法表述时,就发挥一下想象力,编造一些经历。记住:考官是在考查你英语表达的能力而不是观点或常识。

8) 第二部分必须做笔记吗?

不是。考生可以自由选择需不需要做笔记。一些考生喜欢用大脑思考将要表述的话,而另一些认为做笔记有助于他们组织语言并做到表述连贯。

9) 怎样才能确保自己表述的观点是好的?

三个要点通常以"how"或"wh-"开头的问题开始,比如 why, who, when, whether, what 或 which。这些提示将有助你作答。

10) 应该按照这些要点的顺序逐一回答吗?

通常情况下,你可以不按要点顺序任意回答。但是,如果你不擅长组织语言,建议你还是按部就班。一些要点你可能表述得多一些,这是没关系的。

11) 回答时用什么时态?

这要依据问题的提示而定。回答时时态会根据提示的要点而变化。

12) 怎样开始回答?

一分钟的准备时间结束时,考官会提示你开始。首先你要告诉考官你所选择的话题是什么。

13）怎样给考官展示不同的话题词汇？

对你能使用的一些词汇和观点在脑海中有个清晰的认识。考官听的时候会看你是否掌握了和话题相关的词汇。尽可能多地使用相关词汇，不要过度担心犯错。

关于口语考试第三部分的问题：

1）第三部分考查的目的是什么？

考官将让你表述一些和第二部分话题相关的、一般性的但是更抽象的话题。因此第三部分是一个深入阐述。

2）第三部分什么时候开始？

两分钟的回答结束后，考官将引导你进入第三部分，开始会问一些相关话题的更抽象的方面。

3）第三部分如何展开？

问题会逐渐偏难。如果你知道话题是如何逐渐展开且涉及什么抽象观点时，就可以在第三部分深化提升你的回答。

4）回答应该有多长？

考官只会评定你对问题的回答，所以一个既全面又切题并和观点紧密联系的回答是重要的，其中最重要的技巧就是流利度。

5）如何提高表达的流利度？

当你给出一个观点时，尽量用论据去论证它。

6）如何提高发音的分数？

首先声音必须洪亮便于考官听得到。同时发音要尽可能地清晰。要注意重点单词及单词中音节的发音问题，尽量使声音听起来不单调乏味。

7）如何辨识发音中存在的问题？

将这本书中你所做的口语练习的答案都记录下来，然后让老师或母语为英语的人士帮你纠正发音的错误。

六、参加口语考试需要注意的5个小细节

1）保持目光接触

中国考生回答问题时，往往眼睑下垂，这是一种东方人很喜欢的表情，但在欧洲人和美国人看来，这是失去信心的表示。在雅思口语考试时，请与考官保持目光接触，以便交流，这比较符合西方人的沟通习惯。

2）不要自己说英语很差

有些考生英语并不差，但是当他开始自我介绍时却这样自谦，我的英文不是很好……提醒你，即使你的英语真的不好，但是也不要自己说出来，更应该表露出足够的自信。

3）仔细听问题,快速反应

许多考生在考试时,因为听觉不灵敏,不能快速反应。建议你找一个朋友,进行雅思口语测试的现场模式,熟悉环境,这可以锻炼听力和反应,而且还培养了现场的眼神交流等细节。

4）不要不懂装懂

有些考生考试时没有听懂问题,但是他不想公开表示自己没有听懂,所以试着猜问题,试着去回答。这样做存在风险,因为如果问题回答错误,考官会认定你的听力很差。事实上,要求考官重复或确认测试非常正常,所以,遇到这样的情况,你可以大大方方地说对不起,要求考官再说一遍。

5）适当使用停顿技巧

遇到难以马上回答的问题,适当停止非常重要。例如:

问:你喜欢唱歌吗? 答:唱歌? 嗯,我不是很热衷于唱歌,但我喜欢听音乐做些事。看,重复问题,这也是技巧停顿的方法。

七、雅思口语考试回答问题小贴士

雅思口语考试的目的是为了让考生到国外能很好地学习和生活,因此它不仅是简单的对话,还需要考生能回答一些深层次的问题,有一定的英语逻辑思考能力。中国学生在回答问题时,太爱寻求标准答案。比如在一次模考过程中,学生一进门,我一般都会问:"How are you?"而相当一部分学生只会回答:"Fine, thank you, and you?"多一句都不会说。整个上午下来,答案也基本都是 "Fine, thank you." 之类的答案。于是我刻意对后面的考生这样问道:"It's freezing outside, how are you?"可得到的回答依然是 "Fine, thank you, and you?"

这样的回答并没有错误,我们的课本上就是这么写的。但是其实针对 "How are you?"这样的问题,老外的回答可以是多种多样的。例如:

"Great, cheers!"

"Pretty good!"

"I'm okay!"

"Couldn't be better. Thanks!"

"Not too bad. Thanks, yourself?"

透过上面的例子我们不难看出,虽然说评分主要是根据客观语言能力,但打分毕竟还是个主观的过程,如果你说的内容不那么千篇一律而能引起考官的兴趣,那么相比与你同等语言水平的人,你在分数上极有可能会更讨巧。所以建议大家,结合自己的实际情况,找出你自己的特色来,然后把这些特色,灵活运用在更多的主题中。众所周知,雅思的口语考试分为三个部分,分别为 Part 1: Daily conversation, Part 2: Individual long run 以及 Part 3: 2 way discussion. 我们在第一部分就要提供足够"雅思"的答案来给考官留下一个深刻的印象,因为极有可能两个问题之后考官凭经验已经在心中给你打了个分,接下来的问题都只是在证明这个分数而已。

如何使答案与众不同吸引考官呢？答案一定不能千篇一律,准备的时候要注意个性化!

个性化体现在我们回答问题时思维的独特性和立异性。一些有创造性的答案往往可以独辟蹊径,获取高分。下面就口语考试 Part 1: Daily conversation 中的一些问题,为大家举例说明雅思口语考试中的 6 大个性化答题法:拟人答题法、谚语答题法、逆向答题法、细节答题法、迂回答题法和幽默答题法。

方法 1 拟人答题法

Examiner: Do you think cell phones are important for modern people?

Candidate: Speaking of my little girlfriend — Nokia N91, I will have to say: she's like an angel. I had never seen anyone so beautiful before in my life. I was simply hooked on her the first time I saw her. I would always take her along with me wherever I go. My cell phone comes with a digital camera and has turned the vast world into a tiny little village. It's no exaggeration to say: mobile phones make the world go around!

(说到我的女友:诺基亚 N91。我必须说,她就像我的天使。在我生命中从没有遇到过任何人如此美丽,我第一次看到她就被她吸引住了。我走到哪都带着她,我的手机有摄像头,可以把偌大的世界变成很小的村庄。毫不夸张地说:手机让世界转动起来了。)

——这种回答题的方法其实就是把各种实物人格化,赋予这些实物以新的生命。比如:谈到天气问题的时候,我们大可以把北京的沙尘暴变成魔鬼,把鲜花变成美化城市的天使,如此一来,答案自然不会显得枯燥无味。

方法 2 谚语答题法

Examiner: How does the news influence people?

Candidate: News influences people by only reporting certain things and leaving out parts that could matter. One sided news or journalism isn't news but propaganda in my opinion. It's like that good old saying: Some people would rather believe the lies of Satan than the truth of God.

(新闻只是通过报道某一些事情或者报道部分事情来影响人们。在我看来:片面之词的新闻或报道不是新闻而是宣传或导向。就像那句谚语说的:人们宁愿相信撒旦的谎言,也不去相信上帝的真理。)

——恰当地运用谚语可以使我们的语言活泼风趣,增强答案的表现力。谚语有时还可以用来作为说理的根据,证明某种思想观点,起到画龙点睛的作用。英语中的谚语多半在民间口语中广泛流传,表达人们丰富的社会生活经验,处处闪耀着智慧。对于英语谚语的积累,希望考生们能从平时一点一滴做起,时刻留心观察。

方法 3 逆向答题法

Examiner: Do you like flowers?

Candidate: Not at all! I'm a little strange. They remind me of funerals. I like grass.

（一点都不喜欢，我这个人有点怪。鲜花让我想起葬礼，我喜欢草！）

Examiner：What type of music do you like?

Candidate：Well，I am not too fond of music. But sometimes I do like listening to religious music. It gives peace to my mind and joy to my soul.

（我不是特别喜欢音乐。但有时候我喜欢听些宗教音乐，它让我感到安静祥和。）

——逆向思维就是跳出常规，反向而行，换一种眼光，换一个角度看问题。从而发现别人没有发现的新事物、新动态、新思想。逆向思维的作用就是摆脱大多数人的思维模式所做的事情，去寻个别的、新鲜的人和事，从而做到与众不同，出奇制胜，获取高分。

方法4　细节答题法

Examiner：After you graduate, what effect do you think you will have on society?

Candidate：Well，it's a tough question. Let me see. I think I can make an impact in our local community by helping those people around us when we can. May not go down in history, but we may gain a place in someone's heart. That's all I can figure out now.

（这是个难题，我想一下。我认为我可以在社区里帮助那些需要帮助的人，可能不会留垂青史，但至少在一些人心中占有了一定的位置。）

—— 这种答题方法又可以叫做：以小见大答题法。我们在口语中容易犯一些错误：其中之一就是很多同学喜欢说很深刻的大道理，但在雅思口语考试中应该以小见大，举小例子来说明自己的观点。细节答题法的好处是能将"小我"的生活积累和人生体验与社会风云和时代精神连接起来，使难度较大或主题宏阔的写作内容简单化，同时也为真实的、个性化的情感表达找到了一个合宜的方式和路径。"以小见大"常常是以实写虚，以小角度写大境界。

方法5　迂回答题法

Examiner：Do you like your university?

Candidate：Well，it's OK. I don't really like things that are academic and theoretical，but there's great campus life.

（还可以，我不喜欢学术的东西，但是那儿的校园生活很棒！）

——迂回思维就是旁敲侧击，不是正面接触而是绕道而行。思维时做到侧面多、角度多，从其他方面回答考官提出的问题也可以起到相同的效果。

方法6　幽默答题法

Examiner：If you had the opportunity to learn a musical instrument, what instrument would you learn?

Candidate：No，nothing! I am very unmusical! I cannot even sing in tune. Also，instrument's always pretty expensive. If you are really into music, just whistling will do.

（什么也不学，我没音乐细胞，甚至唱歌都跑调儿。而且乐器通常都很贵，如果你真喜欢音乐，吹口哨也一样。）

——口语考试中切忌紧张,如果能在回答时用上适当的幽默,不但能使答案增色不少,还可以让考场气氛轻松下来,何乐而不为?此类的例子不胜枚举,考生完全可以充分发挥自己的想象力来使自己的回答更加生动有趣。

其实,这样的例子还有很多。在此不一一列举。希望通过上面的例句,考生能够清楚一点,也是这里反复强调的:口语考试中,观点无所谓对错。

如果想在口语考试的整个过程中拿到比较高的分数,除了语法、发音、用词和流利度等基本要求外,一定要做到"个性鲜明"。个性鲜明是指我们要有自己的立场观点,并且敢于张扬。任何观点都是可以的,只要能自圆其说,就是成功。有时反而是新奇的答题方法会让考官觉得你个性十足,与众不同,从而引起他们的兴趣。

希望考生在回答问题时,能表现出每个人不同的思维方式,展示出每个人的个性,而不要只会背书。只会背书的学生是得不了高分的。口语考试就是一个考生表现自我的舞台,希望每一个考生都是一个好演员。

当然,不要忘记:任何的技巧都是建立在充分准备的基础上的。因此希望考生平时对口语勤加练习,不打无准备之仗。

图书在版编目(CIP)数据

"低碳雅思"系列.口语冲刺 / 奚挺,吴晟主编.—杭州：
浙江教育出版社,2011.5

ISBN 978-7-5338-8985-2

Ⅰ.①低… Ⅱ.①奚… ②吴… Ⅲ.①IELTS- 口语
- 自学参考资料 Ⅳ.①H310.41

中国版本图书馆 CIP 数据核字(2011)第 064942 号

"低碳雅思"系列

口语冲刺

责任编辑	屠凌云	**装帧设计**	韩 波
责任校对	孔令宇	**责任印务**	陈 沁

◆ 出版发行 浙江教育出版社

（杭州市天目山路 40 号 邮编:310013）

◆ 制 作 杭州富春电子印务有限公司

◆ 印 刷 富阳美术印刷有限公司

◆ 开 本 787×1092 1/16

◆ 印 张 8.5

◆ 字 数 191 000

◆ 版 次 2011 年 5 月第 1 版

◆ 印 次 2011 年 5 月第 1 次印刷

◆ 标准书号 ISBN 978-7-5338-8985-2

◆ 定 价 23.00 元

◆ 联系电话:0571-85170300-80928

◆ e-mail:zjjy@zjcb.com

◆ 网址:www.zjeph.com